Self-Directed
RRSPs

Also by Shirley Woods

Through the Money Labyrinth:
A Canadian Broker Guides You to Stock Market Success

Self-Directed RRSPs

Straight Talk on Making Them Pay Off for You

SHIRLEY E. WOODS

John Wiley & Sons
Toronto • New York • Chichester • Brisbane • Singapore

John Wiley & Sons Canada Limited
22 Worcester Road
Rexdale, Ontario
M9W 1L1

Canadian Cataloguing in Publication Data

Woods, Shirley E
    Self-directed RRSPs

Includes index.
ISBN 0-471-64144-8

1. Registered Retirement Savings Plans.*   I. Title.

HD7129.W66 1995   332.6'042   C95-932765-7

Production Credits
Cover Illustration: Stephen Quinlan
Cover and Text Design: JAQ
Printer: Webcom

Printed and bound in Canada
10 9 8 7 6 5 4 3 2 1

Contents

Acknowledgements

When I write about investments I'm constantly reminded that much of what I know was taught to me by former clients (the same way a student dentist learns by practicing on volunteer patients). To these clients—many of whom are friends—I'm doubly grateful: first, for their loyalty; and secondly, for their high threshold of pain.

One of my most useful sources of up-to-date information on self-directed plans was a series of Nesbitt Burns articles written by Donna Milligan. In addition, Nesbitt Burns kindly allowed me to reproduce several investment graphs and a bond contract for this book. I'm also indebted to RBC Dominion Securities for their permission to reproduce an RRSP statement.

Douglas Cameron of RBC Dominion Securities; Paul Lannan of ScotiaMcLeod; Hugh Bagnell of Richardson Greenshields; Bill V. MacLean of Midland Walwyn; Edwina McFarlane of Nesbitt Burns; Gordon J. Gibson of Lévesque, Beaubien, Geoffrion; and Scott R. MacDonald of Wood Gundy all made important contributions.

As he has done so many times in the past, Gordon Harris of Amarok Systems sorted me out on the telephone whenever my computer got the better of me.

Finally, I must thank Karen Milner of John Wiley & Sons Canada Ltd., who gave me the idea for this book and edited the manuscript.

Preface

A remark by Karen, a career woman in her early thirties, prompted me to write this book. Karen has several retirement plans scattered about Toronto, and was thinking of consolidating them into a self-directed RRSP. But before taking the plunge, she decided to read up on the subject. To her dismay, although she checked the city's leading bookstores, she couldn't find a single book devoted to self-directed RRSPs.

Karen told me about her unsuccessful quest, and remarked that maybe I should write a book on self-directed RRSPs. As she had just finished editing *Through the Money Labyrinth* for me, I knew that this was more than a casual suggestion. My first reaction was: "Who needs another RRSP book?"

Then I got to thinking about it, and visited some bookstores to see what was on the shelves. As expected, I found lots of books on RRSPs. But what surprised me was that they all focused on mutual funds and GICs, and virtually ignored self-directed plans. Added to that, in talking to RRSP investors, I discovered a wealth of misinformation about self-directed plans.

Because self-directed plans offer advantages that GIC and mutual funds plans can't match—such as flexibility, more investment opportunities, and control—and relatively few investors appreciate these advantages, I decided to go ahead and write this book.

Although I was a broker for many years, I no longer have any ties with the investment industry, and have no axe to grind. The object of this book is to help you invest more successfully for your retirement. I hope you will find it useful—and that it may help you to amass a golden nest egg.

S.E.W.
Mahone Bay, Nova Scotia

Myths About Self-Directed RRSPs

There's a lot of misinformation out there about RRSPs in general, and self-directed plans in particular. For instance:

Myth: It doesn't really matter what sort of RRSP you buy, because the main purpose is to get a tax break.

Fact: What you buy matters a great deal. The main purpose is *not* the tax break, but to invest for the future. Therefore, you should be selective, and you should stick with quality.

Myth: A self-directed RRSP is only for the wealthy because of the high cost of the administration fees.

Fact: Fees for self-directed plans are tax-deductible, and average around $125 per year, regardless of the size of the portfolio. If your RRSP is worth $15,000 or more, the fee represents less than 1% of the annual return on your holdings.

Myth: A self-directed RRSP is only for people who want to "play the market."

Fact: If you want, you can play the market with a self-directed RRSP, because this type of plan is flexible. But there's no need to trade frequently and, for the average investor, it's a poor idea to do so. Most successful people make only one or two trades each year.

Myth: Even if you don't play the market, a self-directed plan is risky.

Fact: A self-directed RRSP can be as safe or as risky as you care to make it. As for avoiding risk, only self-directed plans allow you to invest in ultra-safe securities such as Canada Savings Bonds, Treasury Bills, and stripped bonds.

Myth: A self-directed RRSP is suitable only for knowledgeable and sophisticated investors.

Fact: The half-truth in this statement is that self-directed plans are ideal investment vehicles for experienced investors. But they are also suitable for relatively inexperienced people, *providing they have a competent broker to advise them.* While you can assume most brokers are competent, it's useful to know what to look for when selecting one.

Myth: Because you can sell securities to your self-directed RRSP, it's a smart idea to turn your losers into cash by selling them to your plan.

Fact: This is legal, but a stupid strategy for a number of reasons.

Myth: Labour-sponsored venture capital funds are good investments to sell to your RRSP because of the wonderful tax write-offs.

Fact: The tax breaks are undeniable, but the quality of this type of investment is highly suspect. In my opinion, most venture capital funds rank somewhere between a Vancouver speculative stock and a pair of dice thrown against the wall.

Myth: Borrowing to make your annual RRSP contribution is a sound financial strategy.

Fact: Borrowing, in certain situations, does make sense — especially from the point of view of the lending institutions — but it's not always to your advantage.

Myth: Putting your home mortgage into your self-directed RRSP is a clever way of paying yourself.

Fact: Except for special circumstances, putting your home mortgage into your RRSP is a sovereign way to abuse your plan, and won't protect you if you default on payments — you'll still lose your house.

Myth: Managing a self-directed RRSP takes a lot of time, because you have to keep abreast of the market on a daily basis.

Fact: If you're super keen, you might glance at the financial page once a week. On the other hand, if you choose to ignore the market, your broker will normally advise you of developments affecting your holdings. My self-directed plan has a six figure value, and I doubt if I spend more than a couple of hours a year attending to it.

The foregoing "myths," which are widely believed, discourage a lot of people from opening self-directed plans. In this book I'll debunk these myths, and tell you straight from the shoulder how to use a self-directed RRSP to your best advantage. To do this we'll start with the basics, which are covered in the next chapter, and go on from there.

1

RRSP Basics

To best understand the RRSP concept, we'll start at the beginning with the basics. If you're an experienced RRSP investor this chapter may provoke a few yawns—even so, it won't hurt to skim through it to refresh your memory.

RRSP stands for Registered Retirement Savings Plan. Because the full name is quite a mouthful, most people just use the four initials. Years ago I had an eccentric client who twisted these letters into an acronym and always referred to his retirement plan as his "arsep." As he pronounced it with a long A and a soft P, this term never caught on with the public. But by whatever name you want to call it, a Registered Retirement Savings Plan is a great investment vehicle and a first rate tax shelter.

A Registered Retirement Savings Plan is a trust registered with the federal government. When the program began in 1957, the purpose of these trusts was to encourage self-employed people and those who didn't have a company pension plan to set aside money for their retirement. Special tax relief was provided as an incentive, and to compensate for those who already had pension plans. From the government's point of view, the RRSP program made good sense because Canadians who were able to finance their own retirement wouldn't end up being an expense to the federal treasury. Over the years, the program has been refined in a number of ways to make it more attractive to Canadians. These changes have led to phenomenal growth in the number of retirement plans in the past decade.

Today, the government gives two major tax breaks to encourage RRSPs. The first is that contributions—what you put into your RRSP—can be deducted from taxable income. In other words, you don't pay tax on earnings that you contribute to your plan. The second big break is that all the money generated within your RRSP—whether from interest, dividends or capital gains—is sheltered from tax, and thus is tax-free.

While you don't pay tax on your contributions, and your savings within the plan are allowed to grow tax-free, you will eventually have to pay some tax. So an RRSP is technically a tax *deferral* scheme, rather than a pure tax shelter. Here's how it works. When you take money out of an RRSP the amount you withdraw is added to your taxable income for that year. Both the accumulated earnings and your original contributions are taxable. Which is fair enough, because you haven't paid any tax on your contributions, (remember, you deducted them from your taxable income) and all earned income is normally taxable. Not only are cash withdrawals from an RRSP taxed, but so are payments received from an annuity or Registered Retirement Income Fund (RRIF) bought with funds from an RRSP. So, whenever you take money out of an RRSP—in whatever form—you'll pay tax on it. The only exception to this rule is money withdrawn under the Home Buyers Plan (which we'll go into later).

At this point you may wonder: if you have to pay tax on all the money withdrawn from an RRSP, what's the advantage of having one? The answer is that even with the deferred tax, a registered retirement plan produces superior saving results. For this reason, you should consider an RRSP a high-priority investment.

Indeed, *any* plan to supplement your retirement income is worthwhile. All you have to do is look at the financial state of the government today, and then ask yourself whether the social safety net will still be there when you retire. And even if it is, will you qualify for government support? At present there's a "clawback" tax that claws back some or all of the Old Age Security (OAS) payment from middle- and upper-income recipients. Judging by past performance, and the depleted state of the federal treasury, it's reasonable to assume that in the future the Canada Pension Plan (CPP) will also be clawed back. So, unless you're close to the poverty line, when you retire it's unlikely you'll receive any support from the government.

To complicate the problem, there's also inflation to consider. Currently the rate of inflation is low, but it's embedded in the economy, and in the past twenty years has ranged as high as 12% per annum. Without trying to alarm you, let me mention that if your income is $50,000 today, at an inflation rate of only 4% in ten years, you will need an income of just under $75,000 to maintain the same living standard.

Chronic inflation, plus the government's limited ability to fund future social programs, make it prudent to have a nest egg to supplement your retirement income—even if you have a company pension plan. You can build a nest egg by setting aside after-tax dollars or by investing through an RRSP. Of the two, the RRSP is the best way to go.

Let's compare the mathematics of an RRSP and an unsheltered plan. To be conservative, I'll use a personal tax rate of 40%, although the higher the tax bracket, the greater the tax savings with an RRSP. (Forty percent is the approximate rate throughout most of Canada for people with taxable incomes of between $29,591 and $59,179.) In this comparison we'll take $10,000 of pre-tax earnings and buy an 8% guaranteed investment certificate (GIC), with a five-year term. To keep it simple, we won't compound the annual interest. If you buy the GIC outside an RRSP, here are the numbers:

Gross Earnings	$10,000
less 40% tax	–4,000
available for investment	$ 6,000

8% coupon less 40% tax = 4.80% or $288 per year
net income over 5 year term = $1440
Net value of principal and interest at end of term $7440

The same sum invested inside an RRSP produces these numbers:

Gross Earnings	$10,000
tax	nil
available for investment	$10,000

8% coupon less 0 tax = 8% or $800 per year
gross income over 5 year term = $4000
gross value of principal and interest at end of term $14,000

Now assume we withdraw this sum and pay 40% tax on the total Net value of principal and interest after 40% tax = $8400

Although the RRSP is clearly the winner, these figures under-

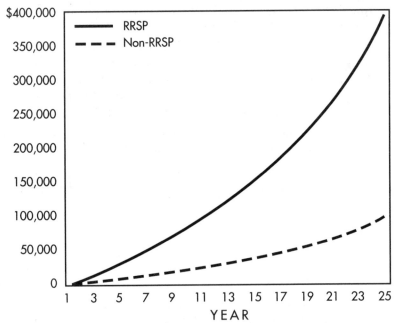

RRSP VERSUS NON-RRSP SAVINGS

Assumptions: Taxpayers in 50% tax bracket; $5000 invested in an RRSP at 8% per annum versus $2500 (after tax) invested at 4% (after tax).

state the case for the sheltered plan because they don't take into account the $4000 refund (or tax reduction) you received when you contributed the original $10,000 to your RRSP. And using a five year term for comparison is another understatement, because the longer the term the greater the performance gap between an RRSP and an unsheltered investment. To illustrate this point, here's a 25-year graph of two people in the 50% tax bracket who annually invest $5000.

Aside from the simple arithmetic, there's another factor to consider in this comparison—the devastation of the tax bite. At maturity, if the RRSP was liquidated and fully taxed, you'd still end up with 82% more in your pocket. From a tax point of view, this is a worst-case scenario, and not a common one. In real life, when an RRSP matures, the holder rarely takes the entire proceeds out in cash. Normally the RRSP is converted into an annuity or a registered retirement income fund (RRIF)—sometimes a combination of both. When a conversion takes place, the retiree pays tax on the annuity payments or RRIF instalments, *not* on the whole wad. With an annuity, the payout is usually a level sum, disbursed at regular intervals. For a RRIF, the payout is on a rising scale, with minimum percentage requirements. Because the balance of a RRIF forms part of your estate, most RRIF holders try to conserve its value by withdrawing as little as possible.

Viewed from any angle, there's no contest between unsheltered savings and funds invested in an RRSP. It all boils down to tax. When you save inside an RRSP you'll be unfettered by tax, but outside an RRSP you'll be handicapped, and play with fewer dollars.

Tax benefits also make RRSPs useful in other ways. Because you can withdraw money at any time (providing it's not a "locked-in" plan), an RRSP can be used for short-term rather than retirement purposes. It isn't the government's intent to encourage short-term saving, but if you follow the rules, it's perfectly legal. And it's quite easy. Indeed, when you take cash out of your RRSP, as long as you leave some assets in the plan you don't even have to collapse it, and it will carry on as before.

Let me play the devil's advocate and mention a few situations that might justify dipping into your RRSP. Heading the list would be cases of genuine need, such as when you've lost your job, and your UI payments have run out. Or you have a cyclical sales job, like real estate, that can be feast or famine. In good years you contribute as much as possible to your plan, and in the lean years you nibble away at it for living expenses. Under these circumstances you've contributed earnings taxed at a high marginal rate, and withdrawn them at the lower end of the scale. So an RRSP can act as a reserve fund against hard times.

Saving high tax dollars and spending them when your income falls can also be done in less pressing circumstances. An unpaid leave of absence, such as a mother quitting her career to have a baby is one example. During the following year or years, when her income is nil, she might take money out of her RRSP to offset household expenses. The same applies to people leaving regular employment to try a new venture (such as starting a small business), or even to academics on sabbatical. The most frivolous strategy—and one that I don't recommend—is to plunder your RRSP to pay for a vacation. I had a client who did just that. He got fed up with the rat race, liquidated all his investments, and sailed around the world for more than a year. The proceeds from his RRSP paid for a good part of this holiday.

Which brings up the question: When you're short of funds, should you dip into your RRSP? Hardliners say you shouldn't under any circumstances. In their eyes, an RRSP is a sacred trust that must never be violated. Personally, I think need should be the determining factor. Tapping your RRSP isn't a cardinal sin, nor will you burn in hell for it. But it's a decision you shouldn't take lightly. Not only will you forfeit savings, and their tax sheltered growth, but *once you take funds out of your RRSP, you can't put them back.* The only exception to this strict rule is money withdrawn under the Home Buyers' Plan, which is covered on pages 60-62.

To sum up, an RRSP is a super investment. It gives you tax breaks while you're saving and, if you let it grow, it will pay off handsomely for you later on. Properly managed, an RRSP is your ticket to financial independence. Especially a self-directed plan—which will permit you to garner the maximum return on your investments.

2 Types of RRSPs: Managed or Self-Directed

At first glance, there's a bewildering array of RRSPs on the market. They're sold by banks, trust companies, mutual funds, financial agents, insurance companies, and stock brokers. And every advertisement implies that this particular RRSP is the best of the lot. However, the situation isn't as confusing as it may appear. Once you cut through the advertising hype, you'll find that RRSPs fall into one of two basic categories. They're either managed or self-directed—and it's easy to tell the difference between the two. Having made this broad distinction, you can then go on to assess the RRSP that's offered.

MANAGED RRSPs

Managed plans, because of their simplicity, are far more common than self-directed plans. Nineteen times out of twenty, when a person says they just signed up for an RRSP, they're talking about a managed plan. When you buy a managed RRSP you pay your money, sign a form, and forget about it. Except for submitting your tax receipt you have nothing more to do, because somebody else looks after your investment. Managed plans are sold by banks and trust companies, as well as by mutual fund companies, life insurance firms, and the myriad agents who flog mutual funds and insurance. Some professional associations and companies also offer managed RRSPs.

Savings Account RRSPs

The savings account is the best seller among managed plans. Again it's a question of simplicity (you don't have to be a mental giant to open a savings account). Safety is also another attractive feature of this type of RRSP. Providing the institution is a member of the Canadian Deposit Insurance Corporation (CDIC), your deposit is guaranteed. RRSP savings accounts are the same as regular savings accounts in that interest is calculated on the daily closing balance and credited monthly, quarterly, semi-annually, or annually. Some institutions offer a progressive or "tiered" rate that increases with the amount on deposit. For example, the base rate might apply up to $4999, with a premium paid on sums over $5000, and an even higher rate for amounts over $25,000. Savings account rates normally "float" up and down with the level of interest rates in general.

When you invest in a savings RRSP your money will be safe, but because rates fluctuate, you won't be able to predict the yield on your investment. You can be certain, however, that the return will be among the lowest in the investment spectrum. In fact, there's a good chance the return will be *less* than the rate of inflation. In this case, although the nominal value of your RRSP will increase, over time the true value or purchasing power will actually *decrease*.

Paradoxically, although it's the most popular, a savings account is one of the worst types of RRSP. Other than as a temporary refuge—when you're caught on the last day of February with no idea of where to put your contribution—there's little justification for a savings account RRSP. A savings account is like a parking lot, in that your money may be safe from the hazards of financial traffic, *but it's not going anywhere*. If you want to reach an investment destination, you must take your money out of the savings parking lot.

Even the most timid soul would be better off with a good money market mutual fund. Money market funds (see Chapter 8) aren't insured, but most hold Treasury Bills and other high grade short-term paper. Thus the risk is minimal, especially for funds sponsored by institutional heavyweights such as the chartered banks and major trust companies. As for liquidity, you can get your money out of a money market mutual fund almost as quickly as you can withdraw cash from a savings account. The clincher, of course, is that money market funds pay much more than savings accounts—often twice the rate.

Term Deposit RRSPs

In addition to savings account RRSPs, the banks, trust companies, and co-ops offer term deposits or certificates of deposit (CDs) for periods of from one month to one year. These deposits usually have a fixed rate, but there are many hybrid variations that combine fixed and floating rates. The liquidity of saving certificates also varies—in some cases you can get your money out without penalty, in other cases you forfeit all or part of the interest, and sometimes they are non-cashable until maturity. Because the rates and conditions differ so much, and they're constantly changing, you should check the market before making a commitment. You can do this yourself by scanning the weekly rate tables in the paper. Or you can contact a financial services broker, and have a professional tell you the best deals available.

Guaranteed Investment Certificate (GIC) RRSPs

Guaranteed Investment Certificates (GICs) rank next to savings accounts in popularity. A GIC is a deposit with a term of from one to seven years—essentially a CD with an extended term. GICs usually have a fixed rate, but the rate can also float, or even be some exotic formula based on an index, such as the Toronto Stock Exchange 300. *As a general rule, the more complicated the rate formula of a GIC, the poorer its performance.*

The main disadvantage of a GIC is that normally you're "locked-in" until it matures. Locked-in means you can't get your money out until the end of the term. When a GIC can be cashed in prior to maturity, there is usually a rate reduction and quite often other penalty charges. Cashable GICs are rare, and you'll have to do some hunting to find an institution that offers this feature.

The word "guaranteed" in guaranteed investment certificate refers to insurance coverage by the Canadian Deposit Insurance Corporation. This insurance covers GICs, savings accounts, and other deposits with a term of not more than five years, to a maximum limit of $60,000 per institution. As a point of interest, the CDIC considers RRSP investments a separate entity for insurance purposes. Theoretically you can have $60,000 in RRSP deposits with a bank or trust company, and $60,000 of non-RRSP deposits with the same institution, and both sums will be covered.

A GIC is perhaps the best of the deposit type RRSPs. Although there's no chance for capital appreciation, if a GIC is purchased at the right time, the interest rate can produce an acceptable return. The time to buy a four- or five-year GIC is when rates are high—say 10% or better. Not when rates are low, because in that case you'll just tie your money up and miss out on the inevitable rise. If interest rates are low, go short-term—one or two years—and don't be sucked-in by some weird formula that's tied to another financial market. A GIC is not supposed to be a speculative investment, so choose "plain vanilla" and settle for a fixed rate. That way, you'll know what your getting, and there'll be no unpleasant surprises.

What happens when a GIC or other RRSP term deposit matures? If you don't give specific instructions, most institutions will *automatically* re-invest or "roll-over" the proceeds of the note for the same term. For example, if you have a five-year GIC, it will be rolled-over for another five years. Which means that if you don't pay attention, your money can be locked into a long-term note when interest rates are low, or into a short-term note when rates are high—just the opposite to what you should do. Allowing a GIC to be automatically re-invested can also frustrate your plans to transfer the proceeds to another RRSP investment, such as a mutual fund, or into a self-directed plan. Institutions normally send out a written notice before a GIC matures, but these can be lost in the mail or inadvertently filed in the wastebasket. So it's up to you to keep a record of your term deposits, and to review them on a regular basis.

Mutual Fund RRSPs

Mutual funds comprise the other main group of managed RRSP investments. It's a huge category, because there are hundreds of mutual funds in Canada. In the early '90s, rising stock prices and falling interest rates resulted in a surge of popularity of funds with RRSP investors. During this period droves of GIC buyers, disenchanted with low renewal rates, switched to mutual funds. A surprising number of these so-called "GIC refugees" thought mutual funds—especially bond and income funds—were guaranteed. When the bond market collapsed and the stock market sagged in 1994, many GIC refugees (as well as other novice fund buyers) were stunned to see the prices of their funds drop, and dumped them. In retrospect, much of the grief could have been avoided if fund sellers had acted more responsibly, and stressed the risks as well as the rewards. The problem, however, also rested with the first-time buyers—who should have investigated before they invested.

Despite these recent melancholy events, mutual funds are still an excellent RRSP investment. One of their virtues, in addition to professional management, is diversification. A typical mutual fund owns securities in many companies—often several hundred—which spreads your risk, and gives you a piece of the action in a variety of situations. Mutual funds run the gamut from being ultra-conservative to roll-the-dice speculations. Depending upon your temperament, and your goals, you can select whatever suits you. The choice is almost unlimited: money market funds, equity funds, bond funds, specialty funds, balanced funds, foreign funds, foreign specialty funds, the list goes on and on. There are even RRSP-eligible balanced Canadian mutual funds that include 20% foreign content—the ultimate in managed RRSP packaging.

Indeed, mutual funds are so well suited to RRSPs, and there are so many types to choose from, that I've devoted an entire chapter to funds later in this book. But for now, if you're considering the purchase of a fund, keep these two cardinal rules in mind: *do your homework, and stick with quality.*

To this point we've looked at managed plans such as savings accounts, term deposits, GICs and mutual funds. Now we'll turn our attention to the other RRSP alternative: the self-directed plan.

SELF-DIRECTED RRSPs

A self-directed RRSP is a personal trust that can hold a variety of investments. Self-directed plans offer important advantages over managed plans, *including better control, ease of management, greater flexibility, and superior growth potential.*

In most cases, a managed RRSP consists of an isolated security, such as a term deposit or shares in a mutual fund. If you have more than one of these plans (and most people sign up for a fresh one every year) this creates both an administrative and a control problem, as well as duplicated service fees. A self-directed plan, on the other hand, acts as a "basket" to hold a wide range of investments. With this type of arrangement you have direct control over *all* your securities, you can more easily *maximize and monitor foreign content,* and you pay only *one* fixed administrative fee (no matter how large the portfolio).

Self-directed RRSPs are offered by banks, trust companies, investment dealers (stock brokers), and some mutual funds. The reporting, accounting, and custodial services of a self-directed plan aren't free. Annual fees vary from about $100 to $200, with the banks and trust companies being at the higher end of the scale, and the brokers at the lower end. RRSP fees, if paid with money from outside your plan, are tax deductible (like your contributions).

Because of the annual fee, you should have total RRSP assets of at least $15,000 before you consolidate them into a self-directed plan. The logic behind this amount is that if you have $15,000, and the annual fee is $150, it will only reduce the annual return of your RRSP by one per cent. Before leaving the subject of fees—and you shouldn't get hung up on it—it's worth noting that some managed plans also charge fees. So if you have several managed plans and you consolidate them into a self-directed plan, you may save managed plan fees in the process, thereby reducing your net cost.

Diversification

There are also a number of important other advantages to a self-directed plan, not the least being the wide range of securities you can own. The broader the selection of investments, the better the growth potential. To illustrate this point I've marked with an asterisk the securities in the following list of RRSP-eligible investments that for practical purposes can be held *only* in a self-directed plan. (I say "for practical purposes" because, in *theory,* all these investments are eligible for both types of RRSP.)

Canada Savings Bonds
cash
cashable savings certificates (CDs)
guaranteed investment certificates (GICs)
Treasury Bills (T-Bills) *
bankers' acceptances *
bonds and debentures (individual issues *)
mutual funds
stripped (zero coupon) bonds *
rights and warrants *
call options *
listed Canadian common and preferred shares (individual
　　issues *)
some unlisted Canadian shares *
mortgage backed securities (individual issues *)
closed-end mutual funds *
debt issued by co-ops and credit unions
labour-sponsored venture funds *
some life insurance policies
certain life annuities
limited partnership units *
shares of some small businesses *
a mortgage on your home *

Control Over Your Investments

Because you make the investment decisions, a self-directed plan offers the potential for better investment returns. Personal control, however, is a two-edged sword. If you gamble foolishly (and I've seen it happen) you can destroy your retirement fund. By the same token, if you ignore your investments, your RRSP can become what is known in the trade as a "self-neglected" plan. But if you use common sense, managing your portfolio can give you a great deal of personal satisfaction. Not only market hot-shots who can pick high flyers, but also conservative investors with no interest in risky stocks, can achieve superior results. Let me give you a couple of examples, taking the two most popular managed RRSP investments, savings accounts and GICs.

If you want a safe and liquid investment and you have a self-directed plan, you can buy Treasury Bills and roll them over as they come due. (You can also buy units in a T-Bill mutual fund, but normally a fund doesn't provide as high a yield because of the mix of maturities and management costs.) As a rule of thumb, Treasury Bills normally pay at least 2% more than a managed RRSP savings account.

Or compare a five-year GIC in a managed RRSP, with a self-directed plan that buys stripped Government of Canada bonds or Canada Savings Bonds. Both the CSBs and the strips are completely liquid—unlike most GICs—and liquidity is important if you need cash for another investment in a hurry, or if you simply want to get out of the market. In addition, strips and CSBs often provide superior yields, while giving you the same or a better credit rating.

In addition to Canadian investments, you're allowed to invest up to 20% of the book value of your RRSP in foreign securities. These investments can be stocks and bonds that trade on approved exchanges, or shares of a mutual fund sold in Canada that holds foreign securities. Foreign content is important because Canadian markets represent only 3% of the world total. Investing abroad provides both a currency hedge and a global opportunity.

The Management Advantage

Which leads us to the management advantage of a self-directed RRSP. It's much easier to manage a single plan, with all your investments in one basket, than to cope with a number of plans scattered around the city in different institutions. Most self-directed RRSP holders receive comprehensive monthly or quarterly statements. The following is a summary page of a monthly RRSP statement:

RBC DOMINION SECURITIES
A Member of Royal Bank Group

STATEMENT OF YOUR RSP ACCOUNT

MAY 31 1995

Page 1 of 2

MS MARY THRIFTY SAVER
123 YOUR STREET
ANYTOWN,
ANYPROVINCE
CANADA
M4X 1CY

Your Account Number: 493-89045-1-3
Trustee: Montreal Trust
Date of Last Statement: APRIL 28, 1995

YOUR ADVISORY TEAM:

Your Investment Advisor:
Doug Cameron
(613) 566-7532

Assistant:
Rosa Brown
(613) 566-7536

Your Branch Address:
Suite 1116, 90 Sparks Street
Ottawa, Ontario
K1P 5B4

Your Branch Manager:
John Bull/Andre Gevry
(613) 566-7500

FOR YOUR INFORMATION:

RBC Dominion Securities is pleased to introduce your new Statement of Account. Should you have any comments or questions about your statement, your Investment Advisor would be pleased to discuss them with you.

ASSET SUMMARY

	MARKET VALUE AT MAY 31	PERCENTAGE OF MARKET VALUE
Cash	$2,491.03	1.51%
Fixed Income	$96,342.00	58.46%
Preferred Shares	$0.00	0.00%
Common Shares	$16,237.50	9.85%
Mutual Funds	$29,104.17	17.66%
Foreign Securities	$20,613.00	12.52%
Other	$0.00	0.00%
Total Value:	**$164,787.70**	**100%**

INCOME SUMMARY

	THIS MONTH	YEAR-TO-DATE
Dividends	$0.00	$92.70
Interest	$11.36	$11.36
Total Income	**$11.36**	**$104.06**

CASH BALANCE

ACCOUNT TYPE	OPENING BALANCE AT APR. 28	CLOSING BALANCE AT MAY 31
Cash	$2,479.67	$2,491.03

CONTRIBUTION SUMMARY

	PERSONAL CONTRIBUTION	SPOUSE'S CONTRIBUTION
First 60 Days	$3,500.00	$3,500.00
Balance of Year	$11,000.00	$11,000.00

FOREIGN CONTENT SUMMARY

Percent of Book Value   10.0%
FOREIGN CONTENT BASED ON BOOK VALUE FOR TAX PURPOSES

At a glance you can see how your investments have fared, what dividends or interest have been paid, the market value of your holdings, the percentage of their foreign content, and the cash balance in your portfolio.

Maximizing Foreign Content

Because of the administrative problem, most managed plan holders don't take full advantage of their foreign content allowance. The rule states that you may invest up to 20% of *each* RRSP in foreign securities, not 20% of the *total* value of your RRSPs. If you currently own a Canadian GIC or other term investment, you can't convert 20% of that to foreign securities (because these investments are usually "locked-in" for their full term). Although some new investment products may help you to skate around the foreign limitation with managed RRSPs, they usually entail an extra element of risk because derivative investments are used. The simplest and best way to maximize your foreign content is to have all your assets in a self-directed plan.

Not long ago I was faced with the problem of a low cost base in my RRSP that restricted the amount of foreign content I could own. I spoke to my broker about it, and he showed me a neat way to increase my cost base. For a nominal fee he arranged for my cash account (my outside account) to buy several Canadian securities from my RRSP which I held at a profit. The following day, my cash account sold the securities back to my RRSP. In doing so, their costs were crystallized at much higher levels, and this increased the cost base of my RRSP. Because foreign content is calculated on the total *cost* of your portfolio rather than its *market value*, and I had increased my cost, this gave me more room for foreign investments. Here's an example of how increasing your cost base works:

total RRSP cost	20% foreign limit	total market value
$100,000	$20,000	$150,000

If $40,000 of the $50,000 increase in value is attributed to Canadian securities, and these securities are sold and bought back immediately, this would crystallize the cost base of the RRSP at $140,000. Look what happens to the foreign content limit.

total RRSP cost	20% foreign limit	total market value
$140,000	$28,000	$150,000

For the average investor—and that means most of us—the best way to invest in foreign markets is through a mutual fund.

The simplest, and often the least risky way to do this is by choosing a balanced global fund. If you're prepared to accept more risk for better growth potential, choose an equity rather than a balanced fund. Conversely, if you want to be more conservative, an international bond fund can provide quite acceptable returns. For cool-eyed speculators willing to accept high volatility in exchange for spectacular gains, emerging growth funds that concentrate on specific areas of the world, such as Latin America or the Pacific Rim, are just the ticket. (But remember, these can also produce startling losses.) Closer to home, I would say that mutual funds are also the best way to invest in the U.S. market. Few investors have enough foreign content room (or the money) to buy a balanced portfolio of individual American stocks, but all of us can buy a piece of an American mutual fund.

Flexibility

Flexibility is another reason for enhanced performance with a self-directed RRSP. Unlike a managed plan, if you have a self-directed RRSP you have all sorts of investment options, and you can be creative in your financial planning.

For instance, you can contribute to your self-directed plan in kind, rather than cash ("kind" means securities or other eligible investments). So, if you're strapped for cash to make your annual contribution, you can use securities you own outside your RRSP. These might be blue chip stocks, like shares of BCE, or high grade bonds. In this connection, a self-directed plan—unlike a managed plan—can hold Canada Savings Bonds. And CSBs are a marvellous RRSP investment. Your self-directed plan can acquire CSBs in several ways: it can receive them as a contribution, it can buy them directly from the Bank of Canada, or it can buy them from you after they're issued.

You can also trade with your self-directed RRSP, buying or selling eligible investments. For example, you may hold a stock that you'd rather not sell, but you need money. Instead of selling the stock on the exchange, you sell it to your RRSP. That way, you continue to own the security (but now it's in your RRSP) and you've raised the cash. Later, you can buy it back from your

RRSP if you wish. Under certain circumstances you can also pledge assets in your self-directed RRSP as collateral for a loan. And, if you have a mind to do so, you can even purchase your own mortgage, and make your monthly payments to your RRSP.

Trading with your self-directed plan doesn't mean that you can rig the prices, or avoid taxes. When you sell or transfer a security to your RRSP you must do so at fair market value. The transaction is deemed for tax purposes as a disposal, which automatically triggers a capital gain or loss. (Unless of course, you transfer the security for exactly the same price you bought it.) Capital gains are taxable the same as if you'd sold on the open market. *However, capital losses don't count—you can't deduct them.* Disallowing capital losses may seem unfair, but it does deter people from dumping their I-hope-it-comes-back-one-day losers into their RRSPs. And if you sell or contribute an interest-bearing investment such as a bond or a GIC to your RRSP, the accrued interest up to the date of transfer is credited to you for tax purposes. For these reasons, it's prudent to consider the tax consequences *before* you put any security into your self-directed plan.

As mentioned earlier, self-directed plans are offered by banks, trust companies, brokers and some large mutual funds. Is there any real difference which type of institution you choose? Yes, there's a tremendous difference, both as to the range of investments available, and the type of service.

What you want is an institution that offers the full range of securities, produces sound research, and makes timely investment suggestions. And a qualified person within that institution who is available to you, and specifically assigned to look after your self-directed plan.

Banks and trust companies fulfil some of these requirements. In a more limited sense, so do a few of the large mutual funds. But when you sit down and compare the various institutions that provide self-directed RRSPs, there's one that clearly has more to offer than the others. The brokers.

For a discussion on brokers, and what you should look for when choosing one, please turn to the next chapter.

3 The Right Home for Your Self-Directed RRSP

Before choosing a home in which to live, you have to know what to look for. This applies also to choosing a home for your self-directed RRSP. You should seek an institution that provides a full spectrum of investments from stocks, bonds, and mutual funds to Treasury Bills and new issues. An institution that produces accurate research, and is noted for its financial integrity. Within this firm you want a well-qualified individual who will look after the administration of your plan, and act as your personal investment advisor.

But how do you go about the search, and where do you start? First of all—before you do anything—you should know something about the financial industry in Canada. Banks, trust companies, brokers, and some mutual funds all offer self-directed plans. But they don't all offer the same features or services.

BANKS, TRUST COMPANIES, AND MUTUAL FUNDS

The chartered banks and the major trust companies tend to stress guaranteed investment certificates (GICs), term deposits

(CDs), and to a lesser extent, mutual funds. Which isn't surprising, because these are proprietary products. Term deposits are safe (when insured by CDIC) and, like mutual funds, perfectly suitable for an RRSP. Bank and trust company annual fees are relatively high, but their transaction charges are reasonable, particularly for banks that trade through their discount brokerage subsidiaries.

Mutual fund RRSPs usually restrict trades to funds within their corporate "family". The self-directed label applies because you can "mix and match" or swap these funds at your discretion. You might, for instance, switch from a stock fund to a bond fund—or from an international fund to a money market fund. Normally there's no charge, or only a nominal fee, to make these changes. Mutual funds are not, of course, guaranteed like term deposits.

STOCK BROKERS

Now we come to stock brokers. Anything a bank, a trust company, or a mutual fund can do, a broker can match. In addition, brokers—especially the large national houses—provide the best research, the widest range of investment options, and the highest calibre of professional service.

For these reasons, you should consider placing your self-directed RRSP with a broker. But not all brokers have identical facilities, and the quality of their personnel also varies. When choosing a broker for your RRSP, you face two problems. First you have to select a good firm, and then you have to find an individual broker within that firm to look after your account. This is where knowledge of the financial industry comes in handy. If you know what goes on in the business, it's much easier to pick the right person to handle your retirement plan.

What's In a Name?

Let's start off by defining the terms "broker," "stockbroker," "broker-dealer," "investment dealer," "underwriter," and "investment banker." We'll take each in turn.

Brokers

A broker and a stockbroker are one and the same. A broker is a person (or a firm) that trades securities on a stock exchange, acting as agent for the client. An agent doesn't own the securities at any time, but makes his money by charging a fee on the way through. Nowadays broker is a generic term that embraces investment dealers and underwriters as well as stockbrokers.

Forty years ago, brokers were simply called "salesmen" or "customer's men." In the fifties, Merrill Lynch moved their brokers' image upscale by calling them "account executives" (a term lifted from the advertising business). Nowadays there are a number of euphemisms for broker, such as "account advisor," "registered representative," "client advisor," and "financial advisor." The last name—"financial advisor"—can imply a number of things because it is also used by mutual fund agents, who are not licensed stock brokers. For simplicity's sake throughout this book, when referring to a salesperson in an investment firm, I will use the term broker.

Before leaving the subject, I should mention that many brokers have "sales assistants" (also called "administrative assistants" or "investment assistants"). These people field phone calls when the broker is on another line, enter trades when he's busy, and look after much of the administrative detail. Providing you know what you want, you can buy or sell securities as easily by speaking to your broker's assistant as by speaking to him directly—and you won't have to wait.

Broker-Dealers

A "broker-dealer" is a very different cat. A broker-dealer trades in promotional stocks and is rarely a member of a recognized exchange. At this writing there are seven or eight of them in the Toronto area. Should you receive a phone call from a person touting a "penny dreadful" the chances are you will be speaking to a broker-dealer. The smartest thing you can do under these circumstances is to hang up. And don't, under any circumstances, confuse "broker-dealer" with "investment dealer" (which would be akin to confusing pimp with priest).

Investment Dealers and Investment Bankers

An investment dealer trades in good quality securities, acting as principal rather than agent. As principal, he owns the securities he sells to you, and when he buys from you he buys for his own account. He makes his money by marking up the securities he sells, and marking down the securities he buys. The difference between these prices and the actual market value is his profit. That is why, when you trade bonds, normally no commission is shown on your contract, (because the fee or commission is tucked into the price). And it's also the reason, when you sell a bond through an investment dealer, the contract normally reads: "Bought from," rather than simply "Sold."

Most investment dealers are also "underwriters." When governments or corporations want to raise money through the sale of bonds or shares, an investment dealer (or a group of dealers) will underwrite the issue. Underwriting means the dealer will buy the entire offering at a set price. Having bought the issue the underwriter then marks up the price by as much as the traffic will bear (his profit) and sells the issue to the public. If he can't sell all the issue, or if he's forced to discount the price, he bears the loss—not the government or corporation. Thus underwriters must have enough capital to accept significant risk, which can run into the tens of millions. On the plus side, underwriting can be very profitable, and it also provides capital for the economy. What is important for you to know is that underwriters of investment grade securities—as opposed to penny stock promoters—are usually responsible people with substantial assets behind them.

REGULATION IN THE INVESTMENT INDUSTRY

The investment industry—because it handles the public's money—is closely regulated by both the federal and provincial governments, as well as by the exchanges and the Investment Dealers Association of Canada. Of these regulatory bodies, the provincial securities commissions have the most teeth, and play the most active role on a day-to-day basis. The Ontario Securities Commission is the model and the trend setter. With a staff of more than two hundred, the OSC sets the standards for all the other provinces, except Quebec (which goes its own way). All the stock exchanges have similar by-laws that apply to their members, but the *enforcement* of these laws varies across the country. The TSE is perhaps the strictest, and the scandal-ridden VSE the most permissive.

Toronto is the country's financial capital, and the home of the largest stock exchange. Montreal also has a major stock exchange, but ranks well behind Toronto in importance. Vancouver has a loosely regulated stock exchange devoted to speculative issues. "Vegas North" and "The world's largest casino" are two of the Vancouver Stock Exchange's more flattering nicknames. (I need hardly add that when investing for your retirement, you should be wary of stocks traded on the VSE.) Calgary and Winnipeg also have stock exchanges, but their volumes are so small that for practical purposes they can be ignored.

The Investment Dealers Association of Canada (IDA) works closely with the provinces and the exchanges. Founded in 1916 at the request of the federal government, the purpose of the IDA—aside from being an industry lobby group—is to ensure ethical business standards and to protect the public. To these ends the IDA monitors the financial positions and the conduct of its members, and if necessary disciplines them. Working in tandem with the provincial securities commissions, the IDA is also responsible for most of the educational courses within the industry (which are far more comprehensive than mutual fund, bank or trust company investment courses). Because membership implies financial integrity and professional competence, it makes sense to restrict your dealings to firms that are members of the Investment Dealers Association.

But what happens if, despite these high standards, a member of the Investment Dealers Association goes belly-up? Should this occur, the Canadian Investor Protection Fund (CIPF) kicks in. The CIPF (which used to be called the National Contingency Fund) is a trust financed by self-regulating organizations in the investment industry, primarily the major stock exchanges and the IDA. In the event a member firm becomes insolvent, the Fund will reimburse a customer for losses related to securities and cash balances up to $500,000. In this connection, coverage of cash balances is limited to $60,000—the same amount as the

Canadian Deposit Insurance Corporation (CDIC) provides—but the Canadian Investor Protection Fund goes on to cover an additional $440,000 in securities for a total coverage of $500,000. If no cash is involved, the CIPF will cover a maximum of $500,000 in securities.

For insurance purposes, self-directed RRSP accounts are considered separate accounts, and each has a maximum $500,000 coverage. Thus a client could have a cash or margin "general" account (separate from his RRSP) that dealt in stocks, bonds, options or currencies, *and* a self-directed RRSP account. Both the general and the RRSP account would qualify for $500,000 coverage, for a maximum total of $1,000,000. Not bad when compared to CDIC.

There are two additional safeguards for holders of self-directed plans. One is that all paid-up securities must be segregated (kept separate) on the books of the broker. The other is that because an RRSP is a trust, all RRSP assets must also be kept *physically separate* from the broker's assets. Surprise audits ensure compliance with these rules. Should a firm get into financial trouble, segregated securities eliminate the risk of mingling clients' assets with those of the bankrupt company.

SMALL FIRMS VS. LARGE FIRMS

By a process of elimination we've narrowed the choice of home for our self-directed plan to a broker who is a member of the IDA. Now we have to decide whether we want to deal with a small firm or a large firm. After we've made this decision, we can zero in and pick the person we want to look after our RRSP.

There are about a hundred firms in the securities business in Canada. Many firms, especially the larger ones, are both investment dealers and stockbrokers. At the bottom of the ladder are small local houses, some of which don't even own a seat on an exchange. Others may have a seat, but do little or no underwriting. As you climb the ladder the size and scope of business operations increases. At the top are the full-service national houses. These firms have numerous branches, are members of the major exchanges, spend millions on research, and have lucrative underwriting connections. Most of these industry leaders, firms such as Nesbitt Burns; RBC Dominion Securities; Lévesque Beaubien Geoffrion; ScotiaMcleod; and CIBC Wood Gundy, are now controlled by chartered banks. At this writing there are only two major firms with large retail sales forces that are still independent: Richardson Greenshields and Midland Walwyn.

The main advantage of dealing with a small firm is personal service. If it's a very small operation, the owner might even look after your account—which, if nothing else, might flatter your ego. However, aside from the personal touch and the satisfaction of dealing locally, there's not much to be said for small firms. For one thing, they don't have the financial strength of the large houses. Nor do they have the trading facilities; often they aren't members of an exchange and have to jitney trades through another broker (which can lead to indifferent service and higher commission costs). Small dealers are also limited in the research they provide and their participation in underwritings.

These limitations ease as the size of the firm increases. While it's nice to root for the little guy, in the investment business, big is beautiful—and the bigger the better. Large firms operate like general stores with stock, bond, mutual fund, commodity, short-term money, and underwriting departments. This provides you, the client, with an investment smorgasbord and the convenience of one-stop shopping. In addition, the big brokers spend millions on research, and participate in many new stock and bond issues. Astute research can make you money, while new offerings can present attractive investment opportunities. However, a few words of caution are in order.

The quality of research varies from broker to broker, and it also varies within each firm. For instance, a house might have the best gold mining analyst on the street, but be realtively weak on utility stocks, or vice-versa. In the bad old days, dealers would sometimes "prime the pump" for a new issue by publishing a glowing research report on the company. Except for junk stock promoters, this doesn't happen anymore. Indeed, by law research reports must state whether the firm has any underwriting or ownership connection with the subject company. Today, if there's a shortcoming in research, it would be the sin of omission—failure to publish a negative report on a company whose securities are underwritten by the broker. But this too is rare. I mention these things because research can be critical to your success, and you should pick a firm with a reputation for accurate, unbiased research.

Underwritings can also be a mixed blessing. New issues (also known as Initial Public Offerings or IPOs) let you get in on the ground floor, and often provide an immediate profit. But not always. New issues sometimes go down, and when this happens it can be a long time before they climb back up to their original offering price. In this connection, the top investment firms invariably have a better underwriting track record than the lesser firms.

The financial strength of the national investment firms is another reason for focusing on them—because the broker you choose (or the institution it appoints), will have custody of all your assets. And, while there are regulations as well as insurance to protect you, it's comforting to know your nest egg is in the hands of a multi-million dollar concern. This is especially true of brokers controlled by the chartered banks. In the unlikely event that one of these subsidiary firms got into trouble, I can't believe it would be allowed to go down the drain.

So, narrowing our search even further, my recommendation is to place your self-directed RRSP with a major investment house. At this juncture, you may wonder why I have given the other players in the game—the trust companies, banks and mutual funds—short shrift. There are two fundamental reasons. The first is that if you want access to the full spectrum of eligible investments, a broker is the logical place to go. Investing for clients is the broker's main business, not a sideline. The second reason is the need, when you have a self-directed plan, for professional advice. A broker is the best-qualified person to provide this service. Let me explain (and I hope you'll forgive me for being frank).

Bank employees are well qualified to engage in banking, but their knowledge of investments—aside from GICs, Canada Savings Bonds, and possibly their own mutual funds—is lamentable. Trust company personnel, except for a handful of people in the investment department at head office, are in the same boat. Most mutual fund agents, while they may know the funds they sell (and sometimes their competitors' products), are also out of their depth when it comes to other investments. As a point of interest, in most provinces you can sell mutual funds after you pass an elementary two-month course. In the investment business, the *minimum* licencing requirement takes three months, and many of the large firms don't let their sales people loose on the public until they've been trained in-house for at least a year.

DISCOUNT BROKERS

One segment of the investment industry that I haven't mentioned is the discount broker. The major chartered banks, led by the Toronto Dominion's Green Line operation, all have discount brokerage subsidiaries. Discount brokers trade securities, especially listed stocks, at discounted rates of commission. The savings can be enormous. How, you may ask, can discount brokers cut prices dramatically, and still make money? The answer is they provide the minimum amount of service. Doing business with a discount broker is not unlike filling your tank at a discount gas bar. You have to know what you want, and you have to do it yourself. Discounters publish very little research, and their sales people don't offer investment advice. Sales representatives for discount houses are essentialy order clerks, because they are neither trained nor licenced to provide advice, and they are paid a salary rather than a commission. From the customer's point of view, it may be a plus that they are paid a salary as it removes any incentive to hustle trades. On the other hand, the absence of an incentive can result in lackadaisical service. My experience—and I have only dealt with Green Line—is that there is no free lunch. When you pay cut-rate commissions, you get cut-rate service.

Professional advice and reliable service are two essential elements of a successful self-directed RRSP, and cogent reasons why you should think seriously before placing your self-directed plan with a discount house. If you deal with a discount broker you won't get any professional advice (and you may not even speak to the same sales clerk twice in a row). As to service, I had three administrative foul-ups with my discount broker in as many weeks. In this connection, when you place an order with a discounter it's prudent to note the precise time of your call, and the name of the person you speak to. Green Line, and I think most of the other discounters, record their phone calls and this information makes it easier to track down an error.

I should also stress—and here I'm including both discount and full service brokers—that administrative glitches with RRSPs can be costly, because they tend to get ignored and come to light long after the fact. If your self-directed plan is with a full service broker you'll pay more in fees and commissions, but someone will always be watching your account. When an administrative or order execution problem arises, that person will go to bat for you.

SELECTING A BROKER

Because full-service brokers have branches across the country, it's easy to find one. The best way to select a particular firm is to ask around. Should you hear good things about two brokerage firms, and you can't make up your mind which one to follow-up, check out both of them by visiting each office and speaking with the branch manager. (If it's a big office, you might have to speak to the retail sales manager.) You can skip this step if you've been given the name of an individual—simply phone that person for an interview.

But let's say all you've got to go on is the name of a firm. When you get together with the branch manager, tell him you're shopping, briefly outline your investment experience, and indicate the type of person you'd like to look after your self-directed RRSP. The manager will, in theory, then match you off with the sales representative who best meets your requirements. (Or, if you're unlucky, he may just introduce you to the most junior broker in the office—the one who needs your business.)

When you sit down with the broker, you're on your own. From now on, you must use your own judgement. Assessing a broker, however, isn't all that difficult—providing you know a little about how brokers operate, and you know the right questions to ask.

Although more and more women are entering the investment business, most brokers are men. (For this reason, rather than saying he/she every time I refer to a broker, I'll use the male gender.) The ratio of men to women is probably 6 or 7 to 1. The numbers are really academic, but what they do indicate is that the brokerage business is no longer a male preserve. So, if you'd prefer to have a woman broker look after your account, there are plenty of well qualified women brokers.

Brokers are notoriously independent people. Although they are full-time employees, most receive no salary but are paid on commission. This means that they start each month with a clean slate, with no assurance of any income. Only those with a strong streak of self-reliance are attracted to this type of arrangement. Brokers' earnings come from commissions generated through trades with clients. (Or as a former colleague used to say, by "turning tricks" with customers.) Commissions are profoundly affected by the market cycle—when the averages are rising they soar; when the averages sag, they plummet. It's a feast or famine type of business.

Brokers depend upon their clients for their income, and do their best to make money for them. This is not because brokers are nicer than anybody else, it's simply good business. When a broker makes money for a client, that person will do business with the broker again (and maybe tell her friends). On the other hand, if the broker consistently loses money for a client, he's likely to lose that customer and harm his reputation.

Everyone has heard stories of unsuspecting folks being fleeced by crooked brokers. Providing you deal with a reputable firm, this is most unlikely to happen to you. Reputable firms play by the rules, and most of the rules are designed to protect the consumer. The worst situation you might encounter is a greedy broker who executes trades solely to generate commission. This is known in the business as "churning" and is prone to occur when the market is in the doldrums and business is slow. Churning is an offense under provincial securities laws, but is difficult to prove in court because not only do the trades have to be instigated by the broker, but the client must also have lost money. Cases of churning are rare because every trade made by a broker is subsequently scrutinized by a corporate Compliance Officer, and when it's discovered, it's nipped in the bud.

I mention the broker's need to make money both for himself and for the customer to illustrate the underlying dynamics of the business. These two goals don't necessarily conflict—the basis of a good trade is when both the client and the broker profit from the transaction. Obviously, you should be careful when choosing someone to advise you on financial matters. But you can safely assume that the vast majority of brokers are honest. And I know from my own experience that brokers take a personal pride in making profits for their clients.

Most brokers are also on the lookout for new customers. Not only do they want to expand their business, but they must replace clients lost through the attrition of death, departures, and disenchantment. This means that when you sit down with a prospective broker, your visit should be welcome.

The choice of a broker is critical to your investment success. Indeed, it's as important as the choice of the investment firm because, for practical purposes, the broker you choose will be your only contact with the firm. To accurately assess your prospect, the interview should be conducted face-to-face, not over the phone. (If you can't see the person you're speaking to, you will miss subtle, but often important, nuances in the conversation.) You should also approach the interview with a positive attitude. This is not a predator and prey, nor a "come-into-my-parlour-said-the spider-to-the-fly" situation. Rather, it is two people meeting in good faith to see if they can arrive at a mutually profitable business arrangement. In a very real sense, you will be interviewing each other.

From the outset, you should be frank. This saves time, and avoids misunderstandings that could come back to haunt you later. You'll have to go over some of the same ground you covered with the manager—your present situation, investment experience, etcetera, and answer a number of personal financial questions. Don't worry about the broker breaking your confidentiality. Brokers treat all conversations as confidential, because it's in their best interest to do so. Not only is money a sensitive subject, but the broker doesn't want anyone else to know that you are an investor (or a potential one), lest a rival try to cadge your account. So you can speak freely, knowing that what you say will stay within the four walls.

There are three fundamental questions you want to explore:

- The first is the competence of the broker.
- The second is whether he understands your investment philosophy and objectives.

- The third is whether the two of you can work compatibly with each other.

The best way to get the answers to these questions is by politely phrased but forthright questions.

As far as competence goes, you can assume that anyone you speak to will be fully trained. What you want to find out is how much experience they've had in the business. Ideally, you should look for a broker who has seen at least one prolonged downturn in the market, otherwise known as a bear market. (If they started in 1990 or earlier, they've been in a bear market.) I mention this qualification because it's easy to make money in a rising market —the real test comes when the averages sink for months on end. A bear market is a harsh teacher, but brokers who survive one learn how to invest conservatively. This doesn't mean you shouldn't choose a novice broker, but if you have your druthers, it's better to pick someone a little further along the learning curve.

I would also try to find out how many RRSP accounts the broker handles, and whether they are of special interest to him. If he doesn't have many self-directed plans, or if he's not particularly interested in this facet of the business, you should look elsewhere.

Something you won't know, until you've done business for some months, is whether your broker has a "feel" for the market. By that I mean the ability to sniff out an investment bargain, or to sense a change in the direction of the market. A few people can do this, but most people don't possess the gift. Formal education has little to do with it—it's more a combination of intuition and common sense. If you're going to trade outside your RRSP it's great to have a broker with a feel for the market. However, if you only intend to open a self-directed plan, this is a luxury you don't really need. Unless you're an aggressive investor, you'll be in perfectly good hands with someone who ignores the short-term swings and takes the long-term approach.

Two significant and related questions are whether the broker understands your investment philosophy and objectives. It may sound odd, but you have to do a bit of soul-searching to establish your own answers before you ask these questions. During my years in the business I spoke with many first-time investors who really didn't know what they wanted from their investments, nor the amount of risk they were prepared to accept. It's fair to assume that most people's RRSP objective is to amass as much money as possible. But how do you want to go about it? Do you want to stay with term and guaranteed investments, or are you prepared to accept an element of risk with equities? If you opt for some equities, what sort of percentage would you be comfortable with? Are you prepared to include individual stocks, or just mutual funds? What about foreign content—do you want to hold foreign investments, and if so what portion of your portfolio?

If you're not sure exactly how you want to structure your RRSP, ask the broker for his ideas. Listen carefully to what he says, because his answer will reveal his investment philosophy, and the manner in which he gives advice. If his ideas are clearly stated, and you agree with them, you've established a basis for a sound business relationship. But if his ideas don't conform to yours—on levels of risk, or the types of investments—you may be on different wavelengths. If you can't reach common ground in your initial meeting, you should thank the broker for his time, and go back to the drawing board.

Now we come to the question of compatibility. Why is this important? Because if you're going to do business with each other, and you can't get along, you'll both be miserable. How can you tell whether you'll be comfortable with the broker? As good a way as any, is to go with your gut feeling. This may sound off-the-wall, but predicting the interaction of personalities is not an exact science. What is essential, however, is that you trust each other.

Trust is critical in the client/broker relationship because there's no written contract, and most buy and sell orders are given verbally. This means that you, the client, and the broker, are both in vulnerable positions. I hasten to add that verbal orders have been used in the financial business for centuries, and the system works just fine. But it does underline the need for mutual trust.

Inevitably, your broker will make a recommendation that doesn't pan out the way you hoped. With an RRSP, which should have a long-term investment horizon, most of these judgement errors will come out in the wash. For instance, a blue chip stock that goes down instead of up right after you buy it (but later recovers), or strip bonds that do the same thing (but eventually mature at 100 cents on the dollar). As long as your broker genuinely cares about your welfare, and he's right more often than he's wrong, you should tolerate his errors. No one is infallible.

You should also feel free to phone your broker if you have a question, or would like his opinion on the market. After all, you're dealing with a full-service firm, and advice is one of the services you're paying for. And don't feel you have to make a trade every time you speak to your broker (but then again, don't phone him just to pass the time of day).

Should things not work out, you can switch to another broker in the same office. Or, in a worst-case scenario, by signing a form (and sometimes paying a fee), you can transfer your entire RRSP to another institution. Thus when you choose a broker, it's not an irrevocable decision.

In most cases, however, the relationship will last for years, and be a source of satisfaction to both parties. Many of my clients developed from being business acquaintances into lifelong friends.

4

Getting Started

O nce you've selected a home for your RRSP, it's easy to open a self-directed plan. All you do is sit down with your broker for half an hour, fill out some forms, and you're in business. At this initial get-together you'll probably arrange for your annual RRSP contribution—you may even write a cheque—and you may also set the wheels in motion to transfer-in one or more managed RRSPs.

Which brings up the question of whether, if you already own stocks or bonds outside your RRSP, you should transfer your regular investment account to your new broker as well. From the broker's point of view, the more assets under administration, the better. Also, the broker is likely to trade an "outside" account more often than an RRSP, and hence make more frequent commissions on it. So the broker would welcome your regular account as well as your self-directed RRSP. From your point of view, there are also advantages. Consolidating your investments makes them easier to manage, and gives you the convenience of one-stop shopping. Finally, you would be a more important customer in the eyes of the broker (some might deny this, but the fact is the importance of an account is directly related to its potential to generate commissions).

If you're not sure what to do, tell your broker that you're going to wait and see how things go with your RRSP before transferring your other securities.

TRANSFERRING Rrsps

When you transfer a managed RRSP (or a self-directed plan) from another institution to your broker, you will likely have to pay a transfer fee. This fee can range anywhere from $10 to $100, with the average being around $25 to $50 for each plan. Don't let these charges deter you. My advice is to bite the bullet, pay the fees, and gather all your investments under one umbrella. In the long run it will save you money (because there'll be no further duplication of fees) and your investment performance will benefit from consolidating your assets. As an aside, some brokers underwrite the cost of transfers, but don't feel hard-done-by if your broker doesn't follow this practice: it's merely a sales ploy to garner more RRSP business. The other thing I should mention about transfers is that they seem to take forever. Practically speaking, you can expect to wait from three weeks to three months for the shift to be completed.

SETTING UP YOUR SELF-DIRECTED RRSP PORTFOLIO

New investors are sometimes intimidated by the prospect of managing their own RRSP. They've heard horror stories about what can happen, and been warned that this is a task for experts. In truth, you don't have to be an expert to be successful. The main thing you need is common sense. That's all very well, you say, but how do you set up your own self-directed plan? I would start by taking a "life-cycle" approach.

Choosing the Right Debt-to-Equity Ratio

A life-cycle approach simply means that you adjust the investment "mix" to suit your age. When you're young you take the most risk, but as you near retirement you become progressively more defensive. Equities carry the most risk and debt securities the least. If we put these two investment categories on a scale, and adjust their proportions to suit your age bracket, it might look something like this:

Age	Debt-to-Equity Ratio
Twenties	all equities
Thirties	15% debt; 85% equities
Forties	25% debt; 75% equities
Fifties	40% debt; 60% equities
Sixties	65% debt; 35% equities

These are arbitrary figures, and should only be used as a rough guide. Your own percentages will depend on a variety of factors, including:

- whether you have a company pension plan
- whether your spouse also has a company pension (and an RRSP)
- the expected value of your home and outside investments when you retire.

If you have a generous company pension plan, and ample outside assets, you can afford to take a more aggressive approach. If, however, your RRSP is your main source of retirement funds, you'll have to steer a more cautious course.

What Investments Should Be In Your Self-Directed RRSP "Basket?"

Once you've established the approximate debt-to-equity ratio, you can focus more precisely on asset allocation. Asset allocation is the balance of cash and cash equivalents, fixed income or debt securities, and equities or stocks in your portfolio. Chapters 6, 7, and 8 cover these individual categories of investments in detail; the discussion below will provide an overview of what kinds of investments belong in each class, and how to balance them in your self-directed RRSP.

Cash or "Cash Equivalent" Investments

The first component is cash or "cash equivalent" (the latter being short-term investments that can be quickly converted to cash). This is the reserve component of your portfolio, and the main requirements are *safety* and *liquidity*. It's not a growth area, nor should you expect high returns. Providing you're paid a competitive interest rate on small cash balances, and you can buy T-Bills or money market funds with larger amounts of surplus cash, your RRSP will be well served.

Fixed Income or Debt Securities

The second asset allocation class is fixed income or debt securities (which includes bonds and GICs). The overriding consideration here is *gross return*. Safety is a priority, but for practical purposes there's no need to restrict yourself to guaranteed investments. At the same time, don't get sucked into buying high yielding mortgages; the reason they have above-normal yields is they are abnormally high risk. Federal and provincial debt, blue chip corporate bonds, and possibly some senior municipal issues, are what you want in your RRSP.

Government bonds and strip bonds both yield more than GICs. You can buy strip bonds as a single maturity, or as a package in a "ladder" of maturities. The ladder concept is useful because when the nearest term matures, you replace it with a maturity at the farthest rung of the ladder. By extending term this way, you take advantage of higher yields.

Because inflation lurks around the corner, you should also consider Real Return strip bonds. When inflation is in check Real Return strips provide a low return, but when inflation breaks out, they really pay off. All the brokers, and most banks and trust companies offer conventional and Real Return strip bonds. It's perfectly feasible, if you want, to buy nothing but strips for the defensive component of your RRSP. They're flexible, liquid, come in all sorts of maturities and amounts, and automatically compound their interest. What more could you want?

Before leaving the subject of bonds, don't forget that Canadian bonds issued in foreign currencies qualify as domestic content.

They provide a currency hedge, but you should also watch out for the coupon. In comparison to ours, most foreign pay bonds offer modest yields. A low coupon—say 2½% to 4%—means that *unless* you have some currency appreciation to make up the difference, you'll forfeit some yield. For this reason, I don't consider foreign-pay bonds a high priority item for an RRSP.

Equities and Stocks

This brings us to the last asset class: equities and stocks. This covers a range of securities from common shares to mutual funds, including a variety of derivative investments like rights and options. No matter how conservative your philosophy, I would strongly recommend that some of your RRSP be devoted to this asset class. But a word of caution. As with any investment—but perhaps more so with equities—a little healthy skepticism is prudent. Do your homework and don't take anything for granted. This applies to existing issues, but is particularly important with new offerings.

Labour-sponsored venture capital funds are a prime example. After you buy shares in a venture capital fund you will be locked-in for at least five years (and possibly until your retirement). If you sell your shares before the end of the prescribed period, you automatically lose your tax breaks. However, there's not always an aftermarket for this type of fund, so you may not be able to sell them, even if you wanted to. And the fund's venture capital investments are also difficult to evaluate, because there's rarely a market for them either. Perhaps the best thing to do with these shares is to consider them like a lottery ticket. They may pay off, but the odds are heavily against you. I think it's a mistake to buy a labour-sponsored venture capital fund. To put one into your RRSP is a folly.

As well as Canadian securities, you should also consider foreign investments. It's widely believed that foreign securities are riskier than domestic ones, but this isn't true. Foreign investments allow you to diversify—spread the risk—across the entire globe. For instance, in the Crash of 1987, while North American markets were falling around our ears, the Japanese market sailed serenely on. Also, because Canada represents only 3% of

the world's markets, foreign securities offer vastly more investment opportunities. *The Financial Post* published a study covering a recent ten-year period that indicated U.S. stocks
outperformed Canadian stocks by more than 25% and international stocks outpaced Canadian equities by 30%. So it makes
sense—for both safety and growth—to maximize your foreign
content. And, regardless of whether they're debt or equity, foreign securities are an excellent currency hedge.

However, there are a few things to keep in mind with regard
to foreign securities. Don't exceed your 20% foreign content
maximum. If you're too close to the limit a single dividend or
interest payment can push you over the line.

Diversifying your holdings spreads the risk. It also increases
the potential for gain, because you'll have more horses running.
This is particularly important with equities. For most investors
the easiest and best way to diversify the equity component of
their RRSP is to buy a good mutual fund. I lean towards balanced
funds, but if you're prepared to accept more volatility, you can
do very well with a straight equity fund. If you have a choice, you
might consider one that has 20% of its assets in foreign securities. But whatever you do—stick to quality.

Managing Your Self-Directed RRSP

If you stick to quality you won't spend sleepless nights worrying
about your portfolio. Indeed, worrying about your investments
won't improve their performance; you're better off taking a
detached view of them. As long as it's sensibly constructed, and
you have a competent broker, your self-directed plan will pretty
well look after itself. All you have to do is keep yourself informed in
a general way. You might, for instance, glance at the financial section of the weekend paper. And from time to time—say once every
couple of months—you might also have a chat with your broker.

Let me close this chapter with one last tip, which I guarantee
will work. When the time rolls around to pay your annual RRSP
fee, pay it by cheque with "outside" money. If you do this, you
can deduct the full amount of the fee from your taxable income.
To be honest, it won't amount to much—around $100—but in
the investment game, every bit helps

5

Rules and Strategies

Studying rules, especially rules concerning taxes and finances, can be boring. In fact, as you wade through this chapter, your eyes may glaze over. But stick with it—we're talking about *your* retirement plan. All of these rules apply to self-directed RRSPs (and many, of course, also apply to managed plans). After we get through the rules, we'll lighten up and look at some investment strategies.

CONTRIBUTION LIMITS

Any Canadian taxpayer who has earned income, and is age 71 or younger, can contribute to a Registered Retirement Savings Plan. So, there's an upper age limit, but no lower age limit—even minors, providing they have earned income, can contribute to an RRSP.

The definition of "earned income" includes salary, wages, fees, commissions, and tips from employment, as well as royalties, grants, rental income, taxable alimony or maintenance payments, and some disability benefits. Earned income is arrived at after deducting employment expenses (including union and professional dues), and the calculation can be quite complicated. For practical purposes, however, most taxpayers can simply refer to their T-4 tax slip, (box 14), and use that figure.

Among the sources that *don't* qualify as "earned income" are: pension payments, annuity payments, RRIF payments, dividends, interest, limited partnership income, and taxable capital gains.

The amount you can contribute to your RRSP varies from year to year, and with the level of your income. The basic calculation is 18% of your earned income to a maximum amount, whichever is the *lesser* figure. As a result of the February 1995 federal budget, maximum limits have been amended as follows:

Year	Maximum RRSP Contribution
1995	$14,500
1996	$13,500
1997	$13,500
1998	$14,500
1999	$15,500
2000	Indexed

From the foregoing table, in 1995 you'll need $86,111 of earned income to reach the limit (i.e., $86,111 x 18% = $14,500). If you have, say, earned income of $50,000, your allowable contribution will be $9000 ($50,000 x 18% = $9000). On the other hand, if you have more than $86,111 earned income, you will be limited to $14,500 regardless of the amount you have earned.

It's also worth noting that in 1996 and 1997 the maximum allowable contribution *drops* from $14,500 to $13,500, which lowers the earned income ceiling to $80,556.

At the top of your Notice of Assessment, just below your name and address, is a box titled in red ink: *Registered Retirement Savings Plan (RRSP) Deduction Limit.* The first line gives your contribution limit for the previous year, and the last line contains the amount available for the current year. At a glance you can tell exactly how much you can contribute.

The box in your Notice of Assessment also shows your "unused RRSP deduction room" at the end of the previous year.

This requires some explanation. You can carry forward, for up to seven years, all your earned but not contributed RRSP allowances since 1991. Thus in any given year you can contribute not only 18% of your earned income, but also as much of your carry-forward as you wish. This is a useful provision, because if you can't ante up the money to contribute for a year or two, you can make it up to your RRSP later. (But don't let this be an excuse to indulge yourself instead of contributing to your RRSP.)

The reason I've stressed contribution limits is that if you exceed them, you'll be penalized in two ways. First, you'll have to withdraw the amount of your overcontribution, which will then be taxed as income. Second, you'll pay an interest penalty of 1% per month for the period the overcontribution has been in your RRSP.

To provide some leeway for honest mistakes, there's an over-contribution allowance. This used to be $8000, but it was changed in the February 1995 federal budget. Starting in 1996, the overcontribution limit will be $2000. In the interim, plan-holders are given a chance to phase-in the reduction by using their 1995 allowance to sop up excess contributions.

RRSP contributions are calculated on the earned income of the *previous* year. Thus, the amount of your contribution for 1996 is based on your 1995 earned income, and is shown in box 14 on your 1995 T-4 slip (for tax payable by the end of April 1996).

Basing your contribution on the previous year's earnings means that you can't contribute to an RRSP the first year you work (or have qualifying earnings). That's the bad news. The good news is that even if you don't work in the second year, you can carry forward your RRSP contribution allowance indefinitely—until the next time you're employed or have qualifying income. Having to wait a year to contribute may seem a peculiar rule, but it's similar to the normal business practice of paying salary at the end of a period of work.

If you're a member of a pension plan or a deferred profit sharing plan (DPSP), the amount contributed to either of these plans must be *deducted* from your RRSP allowance. These contributions, whether made by you or your employer, are collectively known as your Pension Adjustment or PA. After deducting your PA from 18% of your earned income, *the net balance is the amount you can contribute to your RRSP.* Naturally, if you're self-employed or haven't a pension or profit-sharing plan, you can contribute the full 18% of earned income.

Now, before you throw up your hands because you've no idea what's been contributed to your pension plan, there's an easy way to find your PA. It is shown on your T-4 slip (box 52) as well as on your Notice of Assessment (line 5). Your Notice of Assessment is the form you receive when your income tax return has been processed—the one that hopefully says, "We have assessed this return as filed."

CONTRIBUTION DEADLINES

There is also a strict deadline for making your annual RRSP contributions. You can contribute any time from the first of January in the calendar year through the first 60 days of the following year. This works out to a period of 14 months. For 1995, the contribution window is from 1 January 1995, to 29 February 1996. The only people who can't take advantage of the 60-day extension into the new year are those who reach age 71 in the previous year (because their RRSP has to be wound-up by the end of the year they turn 71).

In principle, you should try to contribute to your RRSP as early in the year as possible. This will maximize your earnings because the earlier funds go into your plan, the longer they will have to work, and the more they will accumulate. I could dazzle you with figures and graphs to prove this point, but I'm sure it's self-evident.

In practice, very few people contribute early. About 80% of total contributions are made in the last two weeks before the deadline. This is unfortunate, but there are several valid reasons for our tardiness. Lack of funds is the main one. From the point of view of cash flow, year-end bonuses, maturing savings plans (such as CSBs bought on an instalment basis), and tax refunds all make it more convenient to contribute at the end rather than the beginning of the year.

One way to avoid this is to contribute smaller amounts throughout the year. Most investment dealers will gladly arrange for you to make periodic payments into your RRSP. Layaway plans are neither new nor exciting, but they work. To set one up, just speak to your broker.

TRANSFERRING OTHER RRSP INVESTMENTS INTO YOUR SELF-DIRECTED PLAN

While you are restricted to *how much* you can contribute to an RRSP, there's no limit to the *number* of RRSPs you can own. However, other than theoretically spreading your risk, there's no real advantage to having several RRSPs. The more RRSPs you have the more headaches, and the more fees you'll pay. A sensible solution is to establish a single self-directed plan, and then "get the kiddies off the street" by consolidating your RRSP assets into that plan. To avoid tax, you must fill out a T-2033 form which permits these assets to be transferred "in bond" to your new plan. If you don't fill out a T-2033, but simply collapse your RRSPs and withdraw the money for redeposit, *you will be taxed the full amount of their value.*

To discourage withdrawals some institutions charge penalties (euphemistically called fees), and a few institutions also charge fees for *incoming* RRSPs. Transferring an RRSP is a slow procedure that can take from a couple of weeks to several months. If you are moving a savings account or similar investment, you may also lose some interest while the RRSP is in transit. But don't let these irritations deter you. The procedure is relatively simple—your broker has the forms, and will help you with the paperwork—and it's well worth the hassle. As a point of interest, the Investment Dealers Association's guideline for RRSP transfers is a maximum of 25 days. But this isn't much help to you if you're trying to have RRSPs with other institutions (i.e., banks, trust companies, or mutual funds) transferred into your self-directed plan with your broker. In my experience, the trust companies are the slowest, and there's little you can do about it—except to bug them.

OTHER WAYS OF CONTRIBUTING TO YOUR RRSP

As well as regular contributions and inter-RRSP rollovers, there are several other transfers you can make to your self-directed plan. These come under the heading of Special Contributions, and are in addition to your annual contributions.

Pension Plan Contributions

One of the most common Special Contributions is your share in the company pension plan when you leave an employer. If the proceeds aren't "locked-in," your employer will ask what you want done with them: whether they should be paid out to you (and taxed), shifted to your new employer's pension fund, or transferred to your RRSP. If you wish (and the proper forms are filled out), you can transfer the entire amount without cost or tax liability to your RRSP.

In most cases, however, your pension proceeds will be locked-in. This means you won't have the option of taking cash, or transferring the proceeds to your already-existing RRSP. When a pension is locked-in, the funds must be transferred to a locked-in RRSP or to another locked-in pension plan. Assets in a locked-in RRSP can't be withdrawn or transferred, except to another locked-in plan. When a locked-in RRSP matures (usually at age 65), the proceeds can only be used to buy a locked-in life annuity; you can't take cash, nor can you buy a Registered Retirement Income Fund (RRIF).

Although a recent amendment permits members of federally regulated locked-in pension plans to buy Life Income Funds, locked-in RRSPs are still a financial strait-jacket. Should you end up with a locked-in RRSP as a result of a change in employment, don't contribute any more money to it. This will only exacerbate your problem. Instead, make future contributions to your regular (unrestricted) RRSP.

The reason for locked-in pensions is to ensure holders a retirement income. Patrick, a client of mine, lost his executive position with a large Crown corporation, and ended up with two RRSPs. One, containing his pension contributions, was locked-in, while the other, funded by his severance allowance, was a regular RRSP. Because he was in his late fifties, Patrick found it tough to find another job. He managed to get a little consulting work, but to cover his living expenses he was forced to nibble away at his regular RRSP. Eventually, he went through all of it.

The only reason he didn't collapse his other plan was that he couldn't, because the assets were frozen. This proved a great frustration, and he was furious about it. Until he turned sixty-five, and received his first annuity payment—funded by his locked-in RRSP.

Before leaving the subject of pensions, you should be aware of the "vesting" clause in your pension plan. This states the period of time you must belong to the plan before the company's contributions belong to (or are vested in) you. If you're thinking of a change of scene it's worth checking the vesting clause. You might discover that if you move now you'll lose half your share, but if you hang on for three more months you'll pick up six years of the company's contributions.

"Non-Pension Assets" From an Employer

This brings us to the transfer of "non-pension" assets when you retire, get fired, or choose early retirement. In these cases, the amount of your retirement allowance, severance pay, or golden handshake you can roll into your RRSP is limited. The figure also depends on whether you have earned pension or DPSP benefits. For every year of service up to and including 1995, you can contribute $2000. And, if you haven't any earned pension or DPSP benefits, you can rollover *an additional $1500 for each year before 1989*. There is no contribution allowance for years of service after 1995, but your credit for the previous years can be carried forward indefinitely.

RRSP or RRIF Inheritances

You can also rollover all the assets of an RRSP or RRIF (Registered Retirement Income Fund), left to you by a spouse, a parent or a grandparent, into your *own* RRSP (or RRIF). This rule highlights the importance of naming a beneficiary for your own RRSP. If you don't name a beneficiary, the value of your RRSP will be added to your income in the year you die and taxed at the marginal rate. You can leave your RRSP to anyone you want, but it will be taxed as income in their hands. The only beneficiaries who are totally exempt are your spouse and, in certain cases, a fully dependent child or grandchild. I had a client, who was a doctor, who never got around to naming his wife his beneficiary. He died suddenly and tax ate up more than half his RRSP.

Assets From a Divorce Settlement

Another Special Contribution occurs when there's a division of property—typically in a divorce settlement. In this instance, all or part of the assets in the donor RRSP are transferred tax-free to the recipient's RRSP. This type of division applies not only to legally married couples, but also to common-law partners. (Common-law usually means a couple who have cohabited in a conjugal relationship for a period of at least a year, or less if they have natural or adopted children).

THE IMPORTANCE OF PAPERWORK

Whenever you do a rollover or transfer to your RRSP, make sure to fill out the forms and get a tax receipt. If you fail to do the proper paperwork on a transfer, the amount involved will automatically be added to your income—and you'll pay tax at the marginal rate. Remember too, that you have to declare the transfer for tax purposes the same year it takes place. Transfer forms are readily available from the companies or institutions you deal with, and in most cases they'll do the documentation for you. All that's required on your part is to sign the papers.

By the same token, if you contribute to your RRSP, unless you submit a receipt with your income tax return, you won't get a tax break. The flip side of this rule is that you can go ahead and make your annual contributions, but withhold your receipts. For example, if you expect to be in a higher tax bracket several years from now (for whatever reason), you could hoard your receipts and submit them at that time. This strategy will give you tax relief when you most need it and, in the interim, your contributions will be sheltered from tax.

If you decide to submit a pile of receipts, or use up all your contribution room in a single year, beware of the Alternative Minimum Tax (AMT). The AMT was designed to catch big earners who, through tax sheltering, used to slip through the tax net.

It applies to anyone with earned income in excess of $40,000, and ensures that they pay tax at a minimum rate of 25% *regardless of their deductions and credits.* So don't submit so many contribution receipts at one time that you end up below the AMT line. If you do, they won't help you and you'll have to carry the surplus forward to another year.

Witholding receipts to maximize your tax break shouldn't be confused with deliberately overcontributing to your RRSP. Even when the overcontribution allowance was $8000, this rinky-dink ploy was of questionable value. Now that the limit has been reduced to $2000, you shouldn't even consider it.

BORROWING TO CONTRIBUTE TO YOUR RRSP

If you decide to take out a loan to make your annual RRSP contribution, remember that the interest on the loan—even though it's for investment purposes—is *not* tax deductible. Conventional wisdom says that borrowing to make your contribution is a sound financial practice. Not surprisingly, the lending institutions heartily agree, and offer terms to tempt even the most wary. I've seen lots of calculations that purport to show what good sense it makes. These calculations usually assume that you already have half the amount needed. Then, to repay the loan, they toss in the tax refund on the money you borrow, *plus the refund on the money you saved yourself.* Most examples also project an unrealistic rate of return in your RRSP that matches (or betters) the rate charged on the loan. By flawed logic, and playing fast and loose with numbers, this produces a best-case scenario. But that's not what you should be looking at. What you should consider, before making any financial commitment, is the *worst*-case scenario. My advice is that unless you can pay the loan back within a year, don't borrow to make your contribution.

Borrowing to make your RRSP contribution is a sound practice, providing you can pay the money back quickly, without undue hardship. But being "RRSP poor" because of crushing loan payments makes no more financial sense than being "real estate poor" because of steep mortgage payments, or "insurance poor" because of onerous premium payments.

CONTRIBUTIONS IN KIND

With a self-directed RRSP—and only with a self-directed plan—if you're short of cash, you can contribute in "kind". Kind means investments that are eligible for an RRSP (which we'll get to in a minute). This is a useful provision, but there are certain rules. The first is that the security must go into your plan at its true market value. If it's a Canada Savings Bond, or any other type of bond or investment certificate, the accrued interest must also be added to its value. In turn, you get the tax deduction for the total value of the contribution. But here's something to watch. When a contribution in kind is made, the securities are deemed for tax purposes to have been sold. This means that when you contribute securities you may trigger a capital loss or a capital gain. If it's a capital gain, you must pay tax on it. *However, if it's a capital loss, you can't claim a deduction.*

Contributing in kind is particularly useful when you have a stock that you don't want to sell, but you haven't got the cash to make a contribution. It also works nicely if you have interest-bearing investments (providing you can spare the income). Interest investments flourish in the shelter of an RRSP, while you get the credit for your contribution.

If you're thinking of contributing securities that are down in value, there are two points to consider. The first is one of strategy, the second concerns tax. As an investment practice, you should get rid of your losers—you certainly shouldn't put them in your RRSP. And because you can't deduct your loss if you contribute securities, the obvious solution from a tax point of view is to sell your losers on the open market. This will crystallize your capital loss, and you can then contribute the cash to your RRSP.

MAKING SUBSTITUTIONS

Unlike a managed plan, you can also make substitutions within a self-directed RRSP. Providing you have an eligible security, you can swap it for cash or a security of equal value (or a combination of both). This would make sense if you held an interest-bearing investment outside the plan and a low dividend growth stock inside your RRSP. By switching them, the income security would be tax sheltered and you would have the growth stock, with its dividend tax credit and potential for capital gain (of which, only 75% is subject to tax).

You might also make a substitution to get a low cost "loan" from your RRSP. In this case, you would substitute an eligible security at fair market value for cash. The security would serve as 100% collateral, and you would pay no interest. Strictly speaking, you couldn't call it an interest-free loan because you would forfeit the earning power of the cash in your RRSP. But it's a great deal cheaper than going to a bank. And, when you're in a position to repay the "loan," all you do is buy back the security from your RRSP. (If this procedure has a familiar ring, it's the same principle as dealing with a pawn shop.)

It's surprisingly inexpensive to trade with your self-directed RRSP. When you contribute in kind, or make a substitution with stocks or mutual funds, there are no brokerage fees or commissions. (Some institutions, however, may charge a nominal fee for the paperwork.) You should also note that a substitution, as far as Revenue Canada is concerned, is considered the same as a sale. Again, you will be taxed on capital gains, but you won't be able to claim capital losses.

ELIGIBLE INVESTMENTS FOR SELF-DIRECTED PLANS

Now let's look at eligible investments. But first, a word of caution. RRSP laws change from time to time, so if you're not sure about the eligibility of a specific security, *check with your investment advisor*. With that caveat in mind, here's a list of the Canadian investments that qualify for your self-directed plan:

cash
cashable savings certificates (CDs)
guaranteed investment certificates (GICs)
Government of Canada Treasury Bills (T-Bills)
bankers' acceptances
bonds and debentures
mutual funds
stripped (zero coupon) bonds

rights and warrants
call options
listed Canadian shares (common and preferred)
some unlisted Canadian shares
mortgage backed securities
closed-end mutual funds
listed split shares
debt issued by co-ops and credit unions
labour-sponsored venture funds
some life insurance policies
certain life annuities
limited partnership units
shares of some small businesses
your home mortgage

There are also certain investments that aren't eligible. Here are some of the items you *can't* put in your RRSP:

* foreign currency
* most over-the-counter shares
* foreign stocks not listed on approved exchanges
* commodities and futures
* put options
* gold bullion or coins
* precious metals of any sort
* real estate
* collectibles (art, china, antiques etc.)

If you put something into your RRSP that isn't eligible, or exceed your foreign content limit, several unpleasant things will occur. First, you will have to withdraw the non-qualifying investment. Then you will have to pay tax—at your marginal rate—on its full value (including any appreciation while it was in your plan). And, in addition to the tax, you will be charged a penalty of 1% per month for the period that the non-qualifying investment was in your RRSP.

Foreign Content Allowance

As well as Canadian investments, you are allowed to have up to 20% of the book value of your RRSP in foreign investments. Book value is the actual cost price, including any fees and commissions. (Market value is the price the securities would fetch if sold today.) Suppose, for example, that the book value of your RRSP is $50,000 and the market value is $65,000. In this case, you would be allowed to invest 20% of $50,000—$10,000—in foreign securities. Book value is not difficult to determine providing you keep accurate records, but it's important, if you do a lot of trades, to keep your records up to date.

Because the foreign content rule applies to 20% of *each* RRSP rather than 20% of the total value of all your RRSPs, you should consolidate your RRSPs into a single self-directed plan. This way you can maximize your foreign content, and it's easier to keep track of the precentage limit. In this connection, most brokers provide a running tally of the book values (both for the total portfolio and the foreign content) in their monthly or quarterly statements. Here are some of the securities that qualify as foreign content:

- bonds of certain world organizations (such as the World Bank)
- international bonds with an "investment grade" rating from a Canadian credit agency (such as Dominion Bond Rating Service or Canadian Bond Rating Service)
- foreign mutual funds registered and licensed for sale in Canada
- Canadian mutual funds that hold foreign securities

There is also a huge category comprised of bonds and shares of foreign companies listed on the following exchanges:

North America: New York Stock Exchange, American Stock Exchange, most regional exchanges (except Denver), the National Association of Securities Dealers Automatic Quotations (NASDAQ), and the Mexico City Exchange

Europe: London, Paris, Frankfurt, Milan, Amsterdam, and Brussells

Pacific Rim: Hong Kong, Australia, New Zealand

Determining what securities qualify as foreign content and what securities are considered Canadian content can be tricky. Before you buy anything for your RRSP always check this out. And be careful of foreign companies listed on Canadian exchanges, because they may *not* be considered Canadian content. IBM, which is listed on the TSE, is a good example.

Some Other Wrinkles

Now that we've looked at the investment restrictions, let me mention a few simple—but legal—ways to get around them with a self-directed plan.

The way to own gold is to buy shares in a listed Canadian gold mine, or if you prefer to spread your risk, a gold mutual fund. The same applies to precious metals—several Canadian precious metals mutual funds are eligible for RRSPs. And the same tactic can be used to hold real estate: buy a Canadian real estate mutual fund, or the shares of an individual company (but hurry, before it goes belly-up).

As to the restriction on foreign currency, you can buy Canadian bonds denominated in foreign currencies such as the Deutsche Mark, yen and franc, without even resorting to your foreign content allowance. There are also Canadian mutual funds that hold a combination of Canadian T-Bills and foreign index options. These funds tap into the foreign markets while still qualifying, for RRSP purposes, as Canadian investments.

SPOUSAL Rrsps AND INCOME SPLITTING

To this point, we've been looking at self-directed plans owned by the contributor. You can, however, also contribute to an RRSP owned by your spouse. This type of plan is called a spousal RRSP and has its own set of rules. Contributions made by you to a spousal RRSP are credited to you for income tax purposes, but must be deducted from your personal contribution allowance. Thus, if your allowance is $14,500, the *total* you can contribute to your own and your spouse's RRSP is $14,500.

The purpose of a spousal RRSP is to reduce tax by splitting your retirement income. The tax result—unless both income streams are substantial—will be two relatively low tax rates upon retirement, rather than a single high one.

Your spouse is the beneficial owner of your spousal contribution from the time it's made. But if the funds are withdrawn within the first three years, they will be added to *your* income and *you* will be taxed. After three years, your spouse is liable for the tax consequences of a withdrawal. Should you and your spouse part company, your spouse is the legal owner of the RRSP, even though you may have funded it entirely.

The definition of "spouse" in this instance is a marriage partner, the parent of a child of the contributor, or a person living in a common-law relationship. The definition of living "common-law" is cohabiting for at least a year. A spousal RRSP works best when the spouse has little or no income. Contributing to a spousal plan doesn't make sense if your spouse is a big earner with an RRSP of his or her own. In these circumstances there's no benefit to income splitting. By the same token, a spousal RRSP is only suitable for a couple with a stable, long-term relationship. If you aren't going to stay together, contributing to a spousal RRSP is merely prepaying alimony.

CASH WITHDRAWALS FROM YOUR RRSP

As mentioned earlier, your RRSP can be a source of funds, but you should think seriously before making a cash withdrawal. Once you take money out, you can't replace it—that contribution room is lost forever. Also you will be taxed at your marginal rate on the amount you withdraw, and tax will be deducted *before* the cash leaves your RRSP. The percentage of tax withheld depends upon the amount withdrawn, and whether you live in Quebec or in the rest of Canada. (Quebec withholding tax boosts that province's rates.) Here are the figures:

Amount Withdrawn	Quebec	Rest of Canada
Up to $5000	21%	10%
$5001 to $15,000	30%	20%
$15,001 and up	35%	30%

Remember these are withholding taxes. Your marginal rate may differ, in which case you'll pay additional tax, or get a refund. You can't alter your marginal rate, except by taking money out in a year when your income is low. You can, however, reduce the amount of withholding taxes by withdrawing money in $5000 increments rather than in a single large sum. If possible, of course, you should try to avoid withdrawing any cash from your RRSP.

Rather than withdrawing cash, you can use securities in your RRSP as collateral for a loan. At least, this is the rule. In practice, few brokers will lend on this basis, because they're not in the lending game (except for margin accounts). Banks, trust companies and some co-ops will lend against RRSP assets, but they can be sticky about the collateral. These institutions prefer their own paper (such as GICs or term deposits), or government short-term investments such as Treasury Bills. When you negotiate this type of loan, you'll be taxed on the value of the collateral you withdraw, the same as though it was a cash withdrawal. However, as soon as you've discharged the loan *you can put the collateral back into your RRSP, and claim a tax deduction against earned income for the full amount.*

THE HOME BUYERS PLAN

The only other instance when you can repay a loan from your RRSP is with the Home Buyers Plan. The Home Buyers Plan permits you to borrow from your RRSP, tax free, up to $20,000 for the purchase of your first home. The definition of "home" is a broad one which includes houses (both separate and semi-detached), apartments, condominiums, trailers, and co-op housing. This plan is designed as a once-in-a-lifetime facility, so it's a one-shot deal. To qualify as a "first-time home buyer" you can't have owned a home within the preceding four years, nor can your spouse have owned a home within that period. (As usual, "spouse" includes common-law partners.) The amount you withdraw under the Home Buyers Plan must be paid back to your RRSP, in equal instalments, over fifteen years. Payments start the second year after the year you made the withdrawal. That is, if you withdrew money in 1995, it would be repayable in 1997 (but you have the normal RRSP 60-day extension to March 1, 1998).

Withdrawing the money is simple, providing you use a T-1036 form. Repaying the debt is also easy; all you do is submit a T-1037 form with the annual instalment. You won't of course, get a tax break on these instalments because you already received a tax deduction when you put in the money (and you weren't taxed on the withdrawal). Because the repayment schedule calls for equal instalments, it's easy to calculate the amount of each instalment: simply divide the amount borrowed by fifteen. For example, if you borrowed $15,000, the annual instalment would be $1000.

If you and your spouse are buying a principal residence jointly, then each of you can withdraw up to $20,000 from your respective RRSPs. Indeed, any group of people who can agree upon joint ownership—three friends, for instance—can theoretically each withdraw a maximum of $20,000 for the purchase of their principal residence.

If you don't repay an instalment on schedule it is automatically classed as a withdrawal from your RRSP. The amount of the missed payment is added to your income for the year, and you are taxed on it at your marginal rate. After you miss an instalment your future payments remain the same. If you choose to repay some of the money in advance, you still must make annual instalments, but you can reduce the amount of your instalments. Here's an example:

Borrow	$15,000
Annual Instalments	$1000
Balance owing after 3 years	$12,000
Prepay	$6000
New balance owing	$6000
divided by 12 years remaining	$500
New annual instalments	$500

Some experts say that you shouldn't borrow from your RRSP under the Home Buyers Plan because you'll lose a huge amount in sheltered earnings. This is true, especially over the very long term (and here I'm talking forty years). It's also true that as a policy you shouldn't withdraw funds from your retirement savings. But having said that, the Home Buyers Plan was set up to enable people who had difficulty raising a downpayment to buy their own home. Owning your own home can give you great satisfaction, and if this is the only way to raise the money, I say go ahead and do it. And from personal experience I can assure you that if you make a sensible choice, your home—which is also a tax shelter—can be a hell of a good investment.

USING YOUR RRSP TO FUND YOUR PERSONAL MORTGAGE

On the subject of homes, what about using your RRSP to fund your personal mortgage? You can do it if you want. At first blush this might seem like a super idea—paying yourself those whopping mortgage instalments every month. But let's look at the plan more closely. Here's how it works.

First of all, you can't fudge the mortgage rate, you have to write a mortgage at a competitive rate. For the mortgage to be eligible for your RRSP, it must also be insured by Canada Mortgage and Housing Corporation. And the value of your property will have to be assessed by a professional to ensure fair market value. Then the mortgage will have to be approved and administered by an NHA approved lender. Finally, there will be legal fees. Indeed, everytime you turn around, it will seem that someone has their hand out. Here are some ballpark figures for the basic costs:

set-up fee:	$150 – $250
appraisal fee:	$200 – $250
mortgage insurance:	.5% – 2.5%
administration fee:	$150 – $500
lawyer's fee:	$500 – $1000

To obtain the cash to fund your mortgage it's almost certain that you will liquidate better quality securities. (In this connection, before you do anything, make sure you're not locked-in to GICs or other term investments.) Assuming you can liquidate enough for your mortgage, and you comply with all the other requirements, is it worth the trouble? It depends on how you look at it.

Subjectively, owning your own mortgage can be a comfort, because you're paying yourself rather than some fat-cat lending institution.

Objectively, considering the hassle and costs involved with a self-mortgage, you'd probably be better off going to a commercial lender. That way, you wouldn't tie up a lot of your RRSP assets. To be frank, a personal mortgage doesn't shine very brightly in the spectrum of RRSP-eligible investments. If you're determined to get into the mortgage game, you might consider mortgage-backed securities or one of the good mortgage funds. These investments provide liquidity, geographical diversification, staggered maturities, and professional management.

There's another practical aspect to owning a personal mortgage. Aside from its lack of liquidity, you'll have the ongoing chore of reinvesting the payments—and they come every month. When it's your own mortgage, what happens when you sell the property? (To make the sale you may be required to take back all or part of the mortgage.) Do you want to hold some stranger's mortgage? From the point of view of your RRSP, is this best investment you can own?

Which leads us to another unpleasant eventuality: bankruptcy. Prince Edward Island is the only province that shelters RRSPs from bankruptcy proceedings. Everywhere else in Canada, RRSPs (except for locked-in plans) are fair game. Harking back to personal mortgages, if you went bankrupt and were unable to meet the mortgage payments, it's unlikely you'd foreclose on yourself. But the institution administering your mortgage probably would. Because the Trust Companies Association is petitioning them, it's probable some other provinces will join P.E.I. in extending bankruptcy protection to RRSPs. But only time will tell.

WINDING-UP YOUR RRSP

As mentioned earlier, when you die your RRSP is wound-up or willed to your spouse. If it's wound-up, all the assets are added to the income of the deceased in the year of death, and there's no way to ameliorate the tax blow. If it's left to a spouse or a wholly dependent child or grandchild, the beneficiary can establish an RRSP and the assets can be rolled into the plan tax-free. In this case, there's a ghoulish wrinkle that can be used to further reduce tax. The estate can make a contribution to the deceased person's RRSP for the year of death (which then gets passed on to the beneficiary's RRSP). The effect of the after-death contribution is, of course, to reduce taxable income.

Let me hasten to add that you don't have to die to wind-up your RRSP—you can wind it up at any age you wish. It's your choice. But if you stay the course and avoid the Grim Reaper, when you reach age 71 you *must* wind-up your RRSP.

At this point you have three choices: you can take the cash value, you can buy an annuity, or you can turn your Registered Retirement Savings Plan into a RRIF (Registered Retirement Income Fund). Or, you can choose any combination you want of the three. We'll cover the nuts and bolts of this subject—your retirement options—in Chapter 9, entitled "The Payoff."

RRSP INVESTMENT STRATEGIES

Regretfully, I can't tell you how to make a million by next Tuesday. However, I can suggest a number of ways to improve the performance of your RRSP—and to keep out of trouble. These suggestions aren't particularly new or exciting, but they're worth your consideration.

Contribute Early In Life

The easiest way to create a fat nest egg is to start investing in an RRSP when you're young. Obviously, the longer you contribute and the longer your money has to compound, the greater the eventual amount. But what surprised me was that if you *only* invest during your twenties, *and then don't contribute another nickel,* you will accumulate more than *five* times as much as the person who starts investing the same amount at age thirty and continues to sixty-five.

Contribute Early In the Year

If you're over thirty, don't despair. You can still benefit by being an early bird. Eighty percent of us make our RRSP contribution in the last two weeks of February (of the following year). Yet contributing at the *beginning* of the year provides *significantly* more time for your money to grow within the tax shelter. You've heard this before, and probably seen long columns of numbers covering the next forty years to prove it. I've never been impressed with figures projected into never-never land, and quite frankly they bore me. But a recent Nesbitt Burns calculation caught my attention. Assuming a $10,000 annual contribution and a 10% return, this showed that over just *five* years, if you contributed in January rather than December of the same year, you'd be ahead more than $6000. And that amount is conservative, because very few people contribute in December, most of us contribute the following February.

Contribute Regularly

Practically speaking, however, it's often difficult (if not impossible) to contribute early. We simply don't have the extra money. There are several ways around this problem. Brokers have taken a leaf out of the merchandising book and instituted their version of a Christmas "lay-away" plan, which is an automatic debit system. You sign post-dated cheques or an authorization to debit your account each month or quarter, and the proceeds are paid into your RRSP. The minimum amount, depending upon the broker, can be as low as $100, and there's usually no charge for the service (because they're delighted to have your money). Often this type of plan is tied to the instalment purchase of a mutual fund. This arrangement makes sense (providing there isn't a high commission charge), because your money will go to work immediately, and you will be "dollar averaging".

What's dollar averaging? If you invest the same sum of money in a mutual fund on a regular basis, you will automatically buy more units when the price is low and fewer when it's high. Over a period of time you will accumulate shares in the fund at a relatively low *average* price. That's dollar averaging.

(The same principle applies of course, to the systematic purchase of stock.) Here's an example of how dollar averaging works, using $500 instalments:

	fund price	number of units bought
1st purchase	$12.19	(12.19 divided into $500) = 41 units
2nd purchase	$12.82	(12.82 divided into $500) = 39 units
3rd purchase	$13.51	(13.51 divided into $500) = 37 units
4th purchase	$14.70	(14.70 divided into $500) = 34 units
5th purchase	$13.88	(13.88 divided into $500) = 36 units
6th purchase	$14.28	(14.28 divided into $500) = 35 units
7th purchase	$15.15	(15.15 divided into $500) = 33 units

Average purchase price $13.72

The problem of accumulating enough money for a contribution (as opposed to making it early) can also be solved by systematic saving on your own. This is an old-fashioned idea, but it works. The simplest way is to open a *separate* savings account for the purpose. An even better idea is to sign up for Canada Savings Bonds on the payroll deduction plan. If you choose this route you'll get a much better return than a savings account, and on the first of November you'll have a lump sum to put in your RRSP.

If you can't afford to set aside a certain amount on a regular basis, but you've got an eligible security squirreled away, you can make a contribution "in kind". Remember, however, when you contribute a security to your RRSP it's deemed for tax purposes to have been sold. So you may trigger a capital gain. On the other hand, if you have a capital *loss*, it's not deductible. The way to deal with a loser is to sell it on the market (so you can take the tax loss), and contribute the cash proceeds. Should you contribute a security that you'd prefer to hold outside your RRSP—like a high-tech stock—you can always buy the shares back (at the current market value) later.

The other solution—which is piously recommended by the financial community—is to borrow the money for your contribution. To make it more attractive, many lending institutions offer cut rates for this purpose. My advice is *not to borrow unless you can comfortably repay the loan within the year*. There's absolutely no point in going into long-term hock merely to contribute to your RRSP.

Indeed, the simple way is usually the best way—when you try to be clever, you often get into trouble. Putting your own mortgage into your RRSP is a good example. Some people think it's smart to hold their own mortgage, and that by doing so they're outwitting the lending institutions. In fact, it contravenes a basic real estate principle—that you offload as much debt as possible on *someone else*. Secondly, to raise the money to buy your own mortage you will have to liquidate better, more marketable investments. And, after you get through all the costs, you will likely find that you have saddled a high proportion of your RRSP with an inferior return. Finally, when you sell your residence you may be forced to take back the mortgage—which for all practical purposes will be unmarketable.

While on the subject, should you contribute to your RRSP or pay down your mortgage? There's no pat answer to this question. Like your RRSP, your home is a tax shelter, and down the road can also be used to fund your retirement. But this would involve a reverse mortgage, or selling it. My advice is to make the maximum contribution to your RRSP, and then use the tax refund to pay down your mortgage. That way you can have your cake, and eat it too.

6

Income Investments

There's a great deal more to income investments than GICs and term deposits. Indeed, these bland, non-marketable investments are only the tip of the iceberg. With a self-directed RRSP, you can buy a host of bonds and other debt securities. It's also worth remembering that when you buy a debt security—anything from a term deposit to a Canada Savings Bond—you are *lending* your money. To understand income investments, first you must know how interest rates work.

HOW INTEREST RATES WORK

Interest rates affect all of us. For example, they determine the cost of bank loans, mortgages, rents, merchandise in the stores, and even our utility bills. Interest rates also determine the return on income investments. Because rates are constantly changing, so are the values and yields of these securities. To add to the confusion, prices and yields don't rise and fall in tandem. Instead, when one goes up, the other goes down.

Lots of people, even experienced investors, have a problem grasping this principle. A few months ago I met a man in the Ottawa airport who was waiting for a flight to Halifax. His name was Andrew and, as our plane was delayed for four hours, we had plenty of time to chat. Andrew, a man in his mid-sixties, was a senior consultant to the federal government, and he owned an RRSP worth around $400,000. Eventually, Andrew confessed that he'd never been able to get the relationship between bond prices and bond returns straight. I was surprised that he'd managed his RRSP so successfully with this handicap, and I asked him how he'd done it. Andrew replied rather sheepishly that he paid his son, who was an accountant, to look after his RRSP.

The easiest way to understand the relationship between the prices and yields of these investments—bonds, for example—is to visualize a seesaw. At one end sits the price, at the other end sits the return (yield). When bond prices go up, yields go down, and when bond prices fall, yields rise. The higher the price, the lower the yield, and vice-versa.

What causes interest rates to fluctuate? The short answer is supply and demand, but obviously there's more to it than that. Rather than going into a long dissertation (which I'm ill-equipped to do), let me try to summarize the dynamics. Canadian interest rates are influenced by three major factors: external interest rates, the domestic economy, and the Bank of Canada.

When external rates change, especially U.S. rates, the value of the Canadian dollar is directly affected. If U.S. rates rise, we must raise our rates to prevent a flight of capital, and a decline in the Canadian dollar. (If we don't, international investors will liquidate Canadian investments to buy higher yielding American investments, and dump Canadian dollars in the process.) On the other hand, if the U.S. Federal Reserve lowers rates, we can either sit back and watch the Canadian dollar strengthen, and enjoy an inflow of foreign capital, or we can lower our rates by a similar amount to maintain the *status quo*.

The state of our domestic economy is also a significant factor. When the economy heats up, the demand for money increases, and the cost of borrowing rises. Conversely, when the economy slumps there's little demand for money, and lenders must drop their rates to attract business.

The Bank of Canada—the country's central bank and monetary manager—plays the most important role on a day-to-day basis. Every Tuesday the Bank of Canada holds a Treasury Bill auction. These short term notes are bought by chartered banks, trust companies, brokers and other heavyweights in the financial community. By putting in its own bid the Bank can manipulate the prices, and use them as an instrument of fiscal policy.

The price of the 91-day T-Bill determines the Bank Rate, which is set at 25 basis points above the average yield. (A basis point is one hundredth of 1%.) So, if the average price paid results in a 6.25% yield, the Bank Rate would automatically be 6.50%. The Bank Rate is the rate charged by the Bank of Canada to the chartered banks. In turn, the chartered banks add approximately 1% to the Bank Rate to establish their Prime Rate. The Prime Rate is the rate the banks charge their best customers. I should add that while the T-Bill and Bank rates change every week, the chartered banks usually wait for a significant spread to develop before they change their Prime Rate (and they're always quicker to raise it than to lower it).

TREASURY BILLS

Anything a savings account can do for an RRSP, Treasury Bills can do better. So it's to your advantage to know something about this investment. Treasury Bills normally have a term of one year or less, and are guaranteed by the Government of Canada. They are sold in multiples of $1000, but like all bonds are quoted in one hundred dollar units. Unlike regular bonds, however, they don't pay interest. Instead, they are sold at a discount, and the difference between the discount and par value (100), is your return. Because settlement is the same day or the following day, T-Bills are highly liquid. And not only are they government guaranteed, but *they frequently yield twice and even three times as much as a savings account.*

If you're thinking of buying T-Bills, tell your broker the term that you're interested in, and he'll check his screen to see what the firm has to offer. He may respond by saying something like, "The closest I can come to 90 days is one for 87 days at a 6.55 yield." A few days in the term, one way or the other, makes little difference. The critical figure, and the one you should pay attention to, is the yield. To illustrate the mathematics of a purchase, here are the numbers on a T-Bill yielding 6.55% with a term of 87 days:

Cost of Treasury Bill 98.463   ($984.63)
Proceeds at maturity 100   ($1000.00)
Net return in dollars 1.537   ($15.37)
As a percentage over 87 days 6.55%

When T-Bills are bought for an RRSP there's obviously no tax consequence, but if T-Bills are purchased outside an RRSP the discount between the price and the par value is taxed as interest (not as capital gain).

BONDS

A bond is a promissory note with a fixed rate of interest and a term of from one to thirty years. Interest is usually paid twice a year, by cheque or by coupons attached to the certificate. When the bond matures you receive the face value of the certificate. In the interim, you've been paid "rent" for the use of your money. Bonds, unlike GICs, can be bought and sold, and their prices fluctuate with the level of interest rates.

The Bank of Canada, through its daily interventions in the bond market, also influences longer-term interest rates. Here's how the Bank does it. To lower interest rates the Bank witholds offerings, and bids aggressively for actively traded issues. This push/pull approach drives prices up and brings rates down. When the Bank wants to raise rates, it floods the market with offerings from its own inventory. The sudden surplus forces all the other players to drop their prices, and as bond prices fall interest rates automatically rise.

The Bank of Canada also controls the money supply with a similar strategy. One of the proven ways to stimulate the economy is to make money readily available for investment. Conversely, a useful way to cool the economy is to restrict the money supply (and thereby create "tight money"). To reduce the money supply, the Bank sells large amounts of bonds. When the buy-

ers—Canadian investment dealers and financial institutions—
pay for the bonds, it drains huge sums out of the system. This
tactic is reversed to prime the economy and pump money into
the system. Under these circumstances, the Bank buys heavily in
the bond market, and pays the institutions large chunks of
money. Rigging prices and rates is a legitimate function of the
central bank, whose duty is to protect the value of our currency,
and to keep the economy on an even keel.

The bond market in Canada does a staggering volume of
business—literally billions of dollars each day. It has no premis-
es, but functions "over-the-counter" with a network of phones
that connect one dealer with the other. Trades are based on the
spoken, rather than the written word. In all, there are about 100
participants, including banks, trust companies, mutual funds,
and insurance companies, as well as investment dealers. The
bond market rarely attracts media attention although, on any
given day, its transactions are worth about ten times the combined value of all the trades on Canadian stock exchanges.

Bond Prices and Yields

Rate changes ripple through the market in a matter of seconds.
As they move through the system, prices and yields instantly fall
into line. This continuous process ensures that prices always
reflect current rates. Let's suppose you hold a bond with an 8%
coupon maturing in ten years. If interest rates for ten-year
bonds jump to 9%, no one will want to buy your bond, because
8% is less than the going rate. However, if you *reduce the price*,
you can produce a competitive return—and you'll be able to sell
your bond. Here are the figures:

bond pays $80 per year which at $1000 yields 8%
if the bond is discounted to $935
the ten-year bond with an 8% coupon now yields 9%

This example may need a few words of explanation.
Although bonds are normally traded in $1000 units, the price is
always quoted in $100 units. In this instance, the new price is
93.50 not 935—strange, but it's part of the shorthand of the

investment business. I've also referred to the 8% *coupon,* which is the fixed rate of interest. And finally, the yield to maturity (or return) of a bond consists of the bond's *coupon plus any amortized discount or minus any amortized premium.*

Now let's see what happens to your ten-year bond with the 8% coupon should rates *fall* to 7%. Under these circumstances your bond will be worth *more* (remember the seesaw) and you can sell it for a higher price. Incidentally, when a bond sells above its par value, it's said to be trading at a *premium.* Here are the numbers:

bond pays $80 per year which at $1000 yields 8%
if the price is increased to $1070
the ten-year bond with an 8% coupon now yields 7%

Bonds are sometimes called debentures, and at other times the names are used separately. Technically, a bond and a debenture are two different debt instruments. A bond is secured by a mortgage on a *specific asset* or piece of property. A debenture— which appears the same for all intents and purposes—is *not* secured by a specific asset but by the *general credit* of the issuer. The difference between the two often gets lost in the fog. For instance, Government of Canada medium- and long-term securities are invariably called bonds (i.e., Canada Savings Bonds) when in fact they are debentures. (It's unlikely the government would pledge the Parliament Buildings.) The provinces are also guilty of tarting up their debentures by calling them bonds. However, with the federal and provincial governments it's really academic what they call their debt securities. Where you should be careful is when you get down to corporate issues. Except for blue chip companies, you should always opt for a first mortgage bond over a debenture.

Investors and traders classify bonds as "short-," "medium-" or "long-term" according to the amount of time remaining before they mature. Short-term bonds are those maturing within three years, mid-term bonds from four to nine years, and long-term bonds mature from ten to thirty years.

Term is important because the longer the term, the higher the yield. This principle holds true for all forms of debt, including

GICs and mortgages. There are two fundamental reasons why the yield increases with the term. From the borrower's point of view, the longer the term, the more valuable the loan. From the lender's point of view, the longer his money is out, the higher the risk of insolvency, erosion by inflation, and lost opportunity.

The difference between short-, medium-, and long-term rates is known as the "yield curve." You can make one for yourself by jotting down a selection of government bond yields on a sheet of graph paper. Take the figures from your newspaper, starting with 90-day Treasury Bills and progress out to thirty-year bonds—five or six yields will do the trick. By themselves, the yields won't tell you much; what matters is their relationship to each other. To get your "curve" simply join the numbers with a line. If interest rates are in their regular range, you will get a normal yield curve. It will look something like this:

NORMAL YIELD CURVE

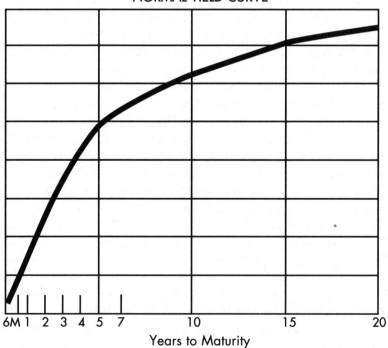

Years to Maturity

On the other hand, if market conditions are out of whack, and short-term rates are higher than long rates, you will get an "inverted" yield curve. Here's what an inverted yield curve looks like:

INVERTED YIELD CURVE

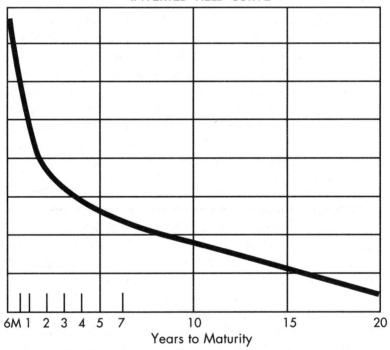

Years to Maturity

An inverted yield curve defies logic (because long-term money is more valuable than short-term money), and this situation is unsustainable. It is resolved in one of two ways: either short rates come down, or long rates move up. Invariably, an inverted curve spells trouble for both the stock and bond markets. For this reason you should be very cautious when an inverted curve develops, and stick to high quality short-term investments, such as T-Bills.

CREDIT QUALITY OF INCOME INVESTMENTS

Credit quality is another factor that affects the return on income investments. Because money gravitates to the least perceived risk, the higher the risk, the higher the return demanded by investors. When assessing credit quality, there are two things to consider: the type of security and the type of issuer.

Type of Security

Theoretically, a Treasury Bill or a Canada Savings Bond is the safest type of security, because both are guaranteed by the federal government, and both can be liquidated within hours. The next safest are "high-grade" (federal or provincial) bonds. The price of these bonds *is not guaranteed on a day-to-day basis, like a GIC, but their principal amount is guaranteed at maturity.* I stress this because some investors confuse Canada Savings Bonds with regular Government of Canada Bonds. High-grade bonds are subject to the discipline of prevailing interest rates, and *go down as well as up.* Indeed, the infamous Government of Canada 4½% bond was "underwater" from the day it was issued in 1958, until it matured twenty-five years later, in 1983. Municipal bonds rank behind most provincial and federal issues, and may or may not be classed as high-grade. Corporate debt—both first mortgage bonds and debentures—are not considered high-grade securities, but can be excellent investments. Lurking in the shadows at the end of the line we have "junk bonds". Junk bonds are issued by corporations with shaky credit ratings, and carry a very high coupon (to compensate the holder for inordinate risk). They are more popular in the U.S., but some Canadian companies have issued junk bonds. These securities are aptly named—from an investment point of view they are junk—and there's no place for them in an RRSP.

Type of Issuer

As I mentioned, as well as the type of security, there's also the credit quality of the issuer to consider. *The stronger the credit of the issuer, the lower the risk, and the lower the rate of interest.* And vice-versa. The credit pecking order is:

1. Government of Canada (and government guarantees)
2. The provinces (and provincial guarantees)

3. Municipalities and districts
4. Corporations

Government of Canada securities always trade at higher prices and lower yields than bonds in the other three categories. The provinces normally yield the next lowest, but credit ratings vary from province to province. Some provinces trade close to the Government of Canada, while others are ranked lower than blue chip corporations. In theory, municipalities rank between the provinces and corporations, but here again there's a lot of variability. Some municipalities have high ratings, while others you wouldn't want to touch with a barge pole. In the corporate area, credit ratings also run the gamut from excellent to dreadful. The major chartered banks and senior utilities are in the top tier and are rated as high as, or higher than, many provinces.

Credit Rating Agencies

Two Canadian agencies, Dominion Bond Rating Service of Toronto, and Canadian Bond Rating Service of Montreal publish credit ratings on a regular basis. South of the border, Moody's and Standard & Poor's also rate Canadian debt from time to time. Ratings are based on an alphabetical system with "triple A" (AAA) being the highest designation. Within this category there are plus and minus graduations from triple A down to single A (e.g., AA+ or AA-). Credit ratings are useful, and can alert you to potential problems, but the bond market makes the final judgement. In the summer of 1995 the market rated the provinces in this order:

Alberta, British Columbia
Manitoba, New Brunswick
Ontario
Saskatchewan
Nova Scotia, Prince Edward Island
Quebec
Newfoundland

Bond Strategies for Your RRSP

If you're buying for your RRSP, I would suggest that you restrict yourself to bonds in the A class. But there's no need to gild the lily. For all practical purposes, a single A rating is as good as a triple A—and you'll pick up yield on the lower rated bond. For example, I recently checked *The Globe & Mail* to see the yields on seven-year bonds. (When comparing yields, always use similar maturities, and start with the Canada issues.) I found that Canada bonds were yielding 7.85% while both Manitoba and the Royal Bank had seven-year issues yielding 8.25%. All three bonds were in the A class: the Canadas being AA+, while the others were single A. So, for a negligible trade-off in security, it would make sense to buy the Manitobas or the Royal Bank and pick up an additional 45 basis points.

There's one other thing that I should mention about quotes in the bond column of your newspaper. These figures are good for comparative purposes, but they are only *levels*—not firm prices. So if you spot a bond in the paper and decide to buy it, don't expect the same price from your broker. The paper has given you last night's closing level, not the price they're trading at today.

How to Judge Credit Yourself

If a corporate issue catches your eye and it's a relatively unknown company, it's handy to have a credit rating. However, if a rating isn't available, there are a couple of elementary ways you can judge the credit yourself. The first thing you want to know is whether the company will be able to service its debt. Bond interest is paid out of earnings *before* taxes. To find out the coverage, get the company's most recent balance sheet and divide the amount of the bond interest into the gross earnings. (If it's a cyclical industry or the earnings have been erratic, it's safer to average the last three to five years.) Should the company have other bond issues outstanding, you must deduct their interest charges *before* making this calculation. Here are the mathematics for a single year:

Gross Earnings	$27,000,000
less interest on existing bonds	–$6,000,000
net available for new issue	$21,000,000
annual interest on new issue	$7,000,000
interest coverage as a ratio	3:1

After you've established that earnings are sufficient to cover the interest, you'll also want to know how well the bond is secured by assets. In a worst-case scenario, you want to be sure there's enough value in the company to pay off the bonds. One way to measure this risk is to find out the amount of assets behind each $1000 bond. To do this, you divide the number of bonds into the company's net worth. Again, if there are other bonds that rank equally or senior to the new issue, you must first deduct their total value. You can ignore preferred and common shares, because bonds and debentures take precedence over them in bankruptcy. Here's a sample calculation:

Net worth	$80,000,000
less existing bond issue	–$20,000,000
net available for new issue	$60,000,000
face value of new issue	$15,000,000
asset coverage per $1000 bond	$4000
expressed as a ratio	4:1

What's adequate coverage for a bond? It depends not only on the company, but also on the industry. For cyclical or junior companies I would suggest a minimum of three times interest coverage, and at least three times asset coverage. Utilities—because of their stable cash flows and effective monopolies—are the safest of all. If you're considering a utility bond you can comfortably reduce these minimum ratios to 2:1, both for interest coverage and asset coverage.

If you stick to federal and provincial bonds you don't need to go through this sort of exercise (and it would be meaningless, anyway) because you can always refer to an agency rating. Rating municipal bonds is also best done by the professionals. Speaking of municipal bonds, my suggestion, after many years in the investment business, is to steer clear of them. Some municipalities have good credit ratings, but most municipal bonds lack marketability. When municipals do trade there's usually a huge gap between the bid and the asked price. This means that you'll suffer whether you're a buyer or a seller. (Metro Toronto bonds are an exception, providing you're willing to trade a minimum of $100,000 worth of them at a crack.) From the standpoint of marketability, federal and provincial bonds are by far the best and tightest traders.

Most people don't want to speculate on the direction of interest rates in their RRSP. But if you have the funds and the inclination, one way to do it is with high-grade bonds. High-grade bonds are readily marketable, which means you can get into them—and out of them—in a hurry. You should also know that the big swings in the bond market occur at the "long end" (the most distant maturities), and low coupon bonds give you the biggest bang for your buck. So a long term combined with a low coupon provides the maximum leverage. However, *I don't recommend that you try to "play" the bond market in your RRSP.* I mention this simply as background information.

New Bond Issues and Your RRSP

Federal, provincial, municipal and corporate bonds are underwritten and sold by investment dealers. When a bond issue is underwritten, an investment firm (or more often a syndicate) purchases the entire issue from the government, municipality, or corporation. The "package" of bonds, which has been purchased wholesale, is then marked up in price and sold to the public. The difference between the dealer's purchase price and the resale price is his profit. Underwriting may seem like an easy way to make money, but there's also substantial risk to it, because the dealer must buy the entire issue outright. If he has to lower his resale price, or if the market turns against him while he's in the middle of selling the bonds, he can take a severe hit. For this reason, underwriting requires good judgement and deep pockets.

Most of the major investment dealers are active underwriters and derive a substantial chunk of their income from it. Some firms have a better track record for underwriting winners than others. In this connection, your broker should screen his firm's underwritings, and only offer you issues that are suitable for your RRSP. And, even if this is the case, it's up to you to exercise your own judgement with a new issue. (Brokers are also salesmen, and don't always stress the shortcomings of their offerings.) If you're unsure whether to buy or to pass up a new issue, quality should be the determining factor. If you stick to quality issues, you won't go far wrong.

Canada Savings Bonds

There are all sorts of income investments to choose from. Canada Savings Bonds have unique features that make them ideal for an RRSP. CSBs pay a competitive rate of interest, there's no cost to buy or sell them, they're guaranteed by the Government of Canada, they're always worth 100 cents on the dollar, and you can liquidate them at any time. You can't, however, make a profit on CSBs, because they can only be redeemed, (you're not permitted to sell them to a third party). The other minor drawback is that CSBs are only offered for sale once a year, from the middle to the end of October. On the plus side, if you buy CSBs outside your plan, you can sell or contribute them to your self-directed RRSP anytime you wish. Because of their liquidity and generous yields, CSBs are especially useful as a cash reserve.

Aside from Canada Savings Bonds, all bonds issued by the federal government fluctuate with the market. This means that you can lose as well as make money on them. The only way you can be sure of getting back 100 cents on the dollar when you buy a government bond is to hold it until it matures. If it's a thirty-year bond, this can be a long wait.

Retractable and Extendible Bonds

With this in mind, some bonds are issued with a retraction feature. A retractable bond allows you to cash in before the stated maturity date. For instance, a bond with a term of twenty years might be retractable after ten years, and again after fifteen years. Thus, if rates settled into a long-term uptrend (as they did from the late fifties to the eighties), a buyer of these bonds would only have to wait a maximum of ten years to get his money back. The same concept, but in reverse, applies to extendible bonds. As the name implies, you can extend the maturity of your bond—to lock in an attractive rate—for a specified number of years. As an example, a bond maturing in 2005 might be extendible for a further five years, to 2010.

Bonds With Redemption Features

So far we've looked at bond options that are to the advantage of the buyer. Now let's look at a couple that benefit the issuer. I'm referring to "call" or redemption features. If a company or a government sells bonds with a relatively high coupon, and interest rates later decline, the issuer would obviously be better off to refinance at the lower rate. But to do that, he has to be certain he can buy back—at a reasonable price—the bonds he sold with the high coupon. For this reason, some bonds are sold with a "call" provision that allows all or part of the issue to be called-in or redeemed on a set-price formula. Normally, the sooner after issue the bonds are redeemed, the higher the price paid for them. In most cases, the premium above par value gradually declines to nil over the term of the bond. The logic behind a declining scale is the earlier the bond is called, the greater the need to compensate the holder for lost income.

The "Doomsday Call" is a recent variation of the redemption feature. A bond with this provision is redeemable at any time, at a price linked to the yield on a Government of Canada bond with a similar term. It works this way: if your bond is called, you receive the *higher* of par (100) or the price of your bond with a yield spread of X basis points over a comparable Canada bond. A Doomsday call with a 30 basis point spread—which is expressed as D+30—is priced to yield 30 basis points over the equivalent Canada bond. For example, if the Canada bond is yielding 7.95%, your bond will be redeemed at a price that yields 8.25%.

Call provisions are common, and you should always check a bond to see if it has one before you buy it. If you don't, and you pay a premium (over par) for the bond, you could end up losing some of your capital. This is what could happen: You see a high coupon bond trading at 104, and you buy it for its compelling yield. A few months later your bond is called at 102, and you not only lose the yield, but also $20 of capital. This may seem like a farfetched example, but you'd be surprised how often investors get caught on bond redemptions.

Strip Bonds

Strip bonds are an excellent investment for your RRSP. A "strip" bond is one that has been stripped of its coupons. Both the stripped bond certificate and the separate coupons are discounted in price to arrive at a discounted yield to their maturity, and sold to investors. Because stripped bonds (and coupons) don't bear interest, but derive their return from the discount, they are sometimes called zero coupon bonds. Depending on the term and the yield, the discounted price of these bonds—which always mature at par—can be astonishing. Here are a couple of examples from a broker's offering sheet. Each package of strips is worth $5000 at maturity:

Security	Discounted Bond Price	Total Unit Cost	Yield
Gov't of Canada due 1 Dec 2005	$40.77	$2038.50	8.76%
Prov of Ontario due 7 Feb 2016	$15.18	$759.00	9.45%

Because most strips are created from federal or provincial bonds, they have a high degree of safety. They are also convenient to own as there's no need to reinvest the interest, it's automatically looked after for you. This gives you a predetermined return on all your capital to maturity, as well as gratifying leverage on your investment. Strips, because the unpaid portion of the amortized discount is taxable, are *not* suited for "outside" accounts—but they work beautifully inside a tax shelter, such as your self-directed RRSP.

Most of the major investment houses (as well as some banks and trust companies) sell strip bonds in "ladders" of maturities. A ladder is a package of strips that mature in succession. The advantage of having a ladder in an RRSP is that you'll always have fresh funds for investment. (Or, if the ladder is in a Registered Retirement Income Fund, you'll receive regular increments of income.) By laddering your maturities, you can continually reinvest at the long end, and pick up the highest relative yields. Here's a sample of a ladder containing five maturities:

Security	Maturity	Yield
Alberta 7%	20 Aug 1997	8.00%
British Columbia 7%	2 Mar 1998	8.12%
Alberta 6%	1 Mar 1999	8.29%
CMHC 8.80%	1 Mar 2000	8.40%
Canada 8.50%	1 Apr 2002	8.50%

When your nearest maturity matures (the Alberta bonds due in 1997), you might roll out to Ontario 8.75% bonds due 1 April 2003, which currently yield 8.98. If you did this at today's prices, you'd replace the lowest rung on the ladder with a strip yielding nearly one per cent more. I should add that the principle of laddering applies to regular as well as to stripped bonds.

Real Return Bonds

Real Return bonds, which also come in the form of strips, are another interesting investment. Real return strips are created from federal government real return bonds. These securities guarantee you a specific return on your money *after inflation*. If you look only at the last few years, inflation protection may not seem much of a priority. But it's worth noting that over the past 20 years the *average* rate of inflation has been more than 6%. Conventional strips provide a predetermined gross return and a fixed amount at maturity. What you don't know when you buy a conventional strip (or any other debt security), is what your actual return will be after inflation. Real return strips take inflation into account and *vary the payout at maturity* to arrive at a net yield. Don't be fooled when you buy a real return investment by what appears to be a low return, because the rate stated is your *net* yield. Perhaps the best way to explain this is to compare a conventional and a real return strip bond. In this example the maturity dates are identical, and the cost of each is $10,000.

Conventional Strip
  yields 8.75%
  worth $18,000 at maturity
  If inflation is at   0%   3.6%   4%   6%
  Real yield to maturity 8.75%   5.15%   4.75%   2.75%

Real Return Strip
  Real yield 5.06%
  If inflation is at   0%   3.6%   4%   6%
  Amount at maturity $14,127 $18,095 $18,590 $21,241

As you can see from this example, if inflation is less than 3.5% you will get a lower return than a conventional strip yielding 8.75%. However, if inflation is more than 3.5% you will be further ahead. In periods of low inflation there's no need to go overboard on real return bonds, but it's always prudent to have some in your RRSP portfolio.

How You Can Use Bonds to Maximize Your Foreign Content

Now let's get back to conventional bonds. The federal and provincial governments, as well as some blue chip corporations (and a few large municipalities), offer bonds in foreign currencies. Although these bonds are Canadian securities, you must pay for them in the currency in which they are denominated— which may be Sterling, U.S. dollars, French francs, Swiss francs, Deutsche Marks, yen, guilders or any other currency. From an RRSP standpoint, Canadian foreign pay bonds are considered domestic rather than foreign content. Therefore you can hold them in your RRSP without resorting to your foreign content allowance. This also applies to foreign pay bonds of certain international organizations, such as the World Bank.

Foreign pay bonds provide risk diversification, a currency hedge, and in some cases a higher return. Interest is usually paid annually. Because an RRSP can't hold foreign currency, the interest must be converted to Canadian funds or used to buy another foreign investment. The same thing happens when Canadian foreign pay bonds mature, you can use the proceeds to replace the bonds, or simply convert to Canadian funds.

MORTGAGE-BACKED SECURITIES

Mortgage-backed securities are another hybrid bond investment. These securities are created by pooling National Housing Association mortgages, which are then sold through investment dealers in minimum $5000 packages. Pooling spreads the risk which, combined with CMHC insurance protection, gives these securities a high credit rating. Despite their high credit rating, mortgage-backed securities always yield from 30 to 80 basis points more than Canada bonds with a comparable term.

Packages of mortgage-backed securities contain "open" and "closed" mortgages. Open mortgages are prepayable, while closed mortgages can't be paid-off before maturity. Closed mortgages also yield less, because an investor can count on their income for the full term. The monthly income from a mortgage-backed security is a blend of principal and interest (at maturity there's no lump sum principal payment). Because you receive varying amounts of principal every month, you're faced with an ongoing reinvestment problem. One solution is to channel the cash flow into a mutual fund instalment purchase plan. This, as as I explain in the "Mutual Funds" chapter, isn't a particularly satisfactory solution. Nevertheless, if you like mortgages, and you're used to dealing with the cash flow, go ahead and buy mortgage-backed securities for your RRSP.

WARRANTS

Sometimes debentures are sold with stock purchase warrants attached as a "sweetener" to induce you to buy them. These warrants are free, and permit you to acquire shares in the company at a fixed price for a given period of time. (See Chapter 7). The value of a warrant depends upon its terms and the outlook for the company. In most cases, warrants attached to bonds have some value (otherwise, they wouldn't be much of an inducement). Therefore, when you buy a bond with warrants, you can either keep the warrants, or sell them on the market.

When you're offered a bond with warrants, remember the warrants have been added as a bonus to influence your judgement. This suggests that you should look at the debenture (or in rare cases, the bond) closely. Crunch some numbers and see how the credit ratios hold up. If they look O.K., what about the rate of interest—is it competitive with similar credit ratings, or have they shaved the coupon a bit? I don't like to sound paranoid, but there are no free lunches, and when there appears to be one you should scrutinize it carefully before you take a bite. This is not to say that warrants are a poor investment, especially if they're free, but it's sensible to determine *why* you're being given them. Once you've figured that out, you can then make an informed decision on whether or not to buy the bond.

CONVERTIBLE BONDS

Convertible debentures also have an equity connection. But in this case, the *entire* debenture can be exchanged for common shares in the company. The exact number of shares is determined at the time of issue, and is stated on the bond certificate. Convertible debentures are often issued by growth companies who plow most of their earnings back into plant and equipment. This policy is good for the company's stock, but doesn't do much for its debt ratios. By issuing convertible debt, down the road the company—through conversion—can expect to raise additional equity capital. Because share appreciation is the name of the game, when you assess a convertible bond, your main concern should be the company's growth potential—not its credit rating.

Convertible bonds, although they normally have lower coupons than straight bonds, always yield more than the dividend on their underlying shares. One advantage of a convertible bond is that if the underlying stock goes up, so will the price of the bond. And, like straight bonds, if interest rates decline, this will also push up the price. Because a convertible bond has *two* props—the underlying stock and its coupon—it will behave better than a regular bond, even if interest rates rise and stock prices fall.

Buying a convertible bond entails considerably more than a simple credit check. The first thing you should do is analyze the company's common shares. Unless you're bullish on the stock, *don't* buy the bond. Then you should look at the conversion rate (the number of shares that can be exchanged for the bond) and note how long it will be in effect. You want a realistic rate, with at least four years in which to convert. The way to figure out the conversion rate is to divide the number of shares into the price of the bond. For example, if a bond is issued at 100, and it's convertible into 50 shares, the conversion rate or price per share is $20 ($1000 divided by 50). Similarly, if you bought the bond in the aftermarket for a premium price of 120, *your* conversion price would then be $24 ($1200 divided by 50).

Another thing to watch for is whether the bond is callable (especially if you'll be paying a significant premium). This is important because the bond could be called for a price *less* than the one you paid. However, if your bond is redeemed you'll always be given a chance to convert into common shares—so the price of the underlying stock is critical. Let's say you bought the bond we just mentioned for 120, and it's called at 104. This doesn't mean you're automatically going to lose 16 points or $160 per bond. If the stock is trading at $24, you won't lose a cent because you can convert and sell the shares (50 x $24 = $1200) on the market. (In reality you'd probably lose a few bucks, because convertible bonds almost always trade at a premium to their conversion value.)

This leads us to the calculation of the premium and the payback period. The premium is the amount you pay for the bond, expressed as a percentage, above the market value of the underlying stock. The payback period is the time it takes to recoup the premium through the bond's yield in excess of the stock yield. Whether the premium is reasonable depends upon the length of the payback period—thus, the two calculations are contingent upon each other.

Let's say you're looking at a convertible bond priced at 114. The bond yields 6.25% and is callable at 103.50 in 1998. It is convertible into 50 shares of common stock until 2002. The common is currently trading at 21.50 and yields 1%. To figure out the premium, multiply the number of shares by their market price and deduct the total from the price of the bond:

50 shares x $21.50 = $1075 – $1140 = $75 premium
expressed as a percentage, the premium = 6.6%

To calculate the payback period, take the difference between the stock and the bond yields, and divide it into the premium:

6.25% − 1% = 5.25% divided into 6.6% premium = 1.3 years

As the payback period is *less than two years* the premium on this bond appears reasonable. Strictly from a price point of view, you could go ahead and buy the bond.

To sum up, convertible bonds allow you to play the common stock of a company with less risk than if you held the shares. Convertible bonds are also safer in the event of bankruptcy, because they have a prior call on the company's assets. If the company's shares go up, the conversion feature ensures that the bond appreciates at a similar rate to the common stock. And while you're waiting for the stock to move, convertible bonds provide a much better yield than their underlying shares. All things considered, convertible bonds are an ideal investment for your self-directed RRSP.

But, just so that you don't go overboard, I'll leave you with a cautionary tale. Some years ago, a client of one of my colleagues thought that Campeau Corporation—despite the company having indigestion from taking over several American retailers—was the best thing since sliced bread. Indeed, this client was sure that Campeau would not only overcome its problems, but its shares would soar to undreamed-of heights. So he liquidated all the investments in his RRSP—all the high-grade bonds and all the blue chip stocks—and put the whole wad into Campeau convertible debentures. Two years later, Campeau Corporation went belly-up.

BOND CONTRACTS

Bond contracts (the written confirmation you receive after making a bond trade) differ from stock contracts. The first thing you'll notice is that no commission is shown. It's there, but you won't see it because it's added or subtracted from the price. (Bond commissions rise as the term lengthens, but are substantially lower than stock or mutual fund commissions.) You'll also notice an entry crediting or debiting you with accrued interest.

NESBITT BURNS

Member of the Bank of Montreal Group of Companies
Membre du groupe de sociétés de la Banque de Montréal

WE CONFIRM THIS TRANSACTION SUBJECT TO THE AGREEMENT ON THE REVERSE SIDE / NOUS CONFIRMONS CETTE TRANSACTION EN VERTU DES CONDITIONS DE L'ACCORD INDIQUÉ AU VERSO

OFFICES IN PRINCIPAL CANADIAN CITIES
BUREAUX DANS LES PRINCIPALES VILLES CANADIENNES

APRIL 21, 1995

SETTLEMENT DATE
APRIL 28, 1995

AS PRINCIPAL, WE TODAY CONFIRM THE FOLLOWING SALE TO YOU

25,000 BOUGHT

ONTARIO HYDRO GLOBAL
ISIN # CAGB3078FW 1
DUE 03/31/1998 0.7250% MS 31
INT DAYS   28, NEXT CPN 96/09/30

FOR SETTLEMENT IN THIS OFFICE

GROSS AMOUNT $24,562.50

INTEREST   139.04

SUB TOTAL $24,701.54

NET AMOUNT $24,701.54

REMITTANCE SHOULD INCLUDE YOUR ACCOUNT NUMBER
VEUILLEZ INSCRIRE LE NUMÉRO DE VOTRE COMPTE SUR VOTRE CHÈQUE

ACCOUNT NO.
Nº DE COMPTE
123-45678-90

TYPE:
GENRE:

INVESTMENT ADVISOR
CONSEILLER FINANCIER
JOHN DOE
TEL.   ABC

I.A. NO.
Nº C.F.

INTERNAL CODES

CUSIP

SECURITY NO.
Nº DU TITRE
ORDER NO.
Nº DE L'ORDRE
REFERENCE

MR. JOHN SMITH
P.O. Box 2408
HALIFAX N.S.
B3J 3E4

SAMPLE ONLY

PLEASE RETAIN THIS CONTRACT FOR INCOME TAX PURPOSES / VEUILLEZ CONSERVER LE PRÉSENT CONTRAT POUR FINS D'IMPÔT

When you buy a bond you are charged accrued interest from the day the last interest payment was made. This makes sense, because the former owner held the bond during this period and should get the interest. Later, when you receive the *full* amount of the next interest instalment, this charge will cancel out. Conversely, if you sell a bond, you'll be paid accrued interest. And, because the dealer is acting as a principal rather than as an agent, when you sell bonds the contract will say "bought from you." When you buy bonds, instead of saying "bought" the contract will say "sold to you." On the previous page is a sample bond contract to illustrate these points.

A CLOSING TIP

I'll close this chapter with two suggestions. The time to buy long-term bonds is when interest rates are high—when everybody's complaining about the cost of mortgages and bank loans. The time to stick to short-term investments is when rates are low—when people are grumbling about the lousy interest on their GIC renewals. If you follow this simple advice you'll never get trapped in low yielding bonds, and you'll consistently lock-in high rates of return.

7

Equity Investments

I think everyone—regardless of their age—should have an equity component in their RRSP. I say this because common stocks are an excellent hedge against inflation, and inflation is always with us.

Stocks or shares are riskier than bonds and GICs, but they can also be more rewarding. If someone tells you they've made money in the market, 99 times out of a 100, they've made it on a high flying stock, not on bonds. And it may suprise you to know that Canadian insurance companies hold billions of dollars worth of blue chip stocks.

COMMON STOCKS

When you buy common stock, you become a part owner of the company. As a part owner you have a say in the management, you share in the earnings and, in the event of bankruptcy, you stand last in the line of creditors. (When you buy a bond or GIC you're a preferred creditor, but you don't have any equity in the investment.) Common shareholders receive their slice of the profits through dividends. Unlike interest, which is a fixed obligation, dividends are paid at the discretion of the board of directors. Normally each common share carries one vote, so your say in the management of the company is proportionate to the amount of stock you hold. Should the business fail, you may not get any money back, but if the company prospers, the value of your shares will increase, and so will the amount of your dividends.

Most people buy common stocks for growth, not income. This makes sense, because many of the best growth stocks don't pay any dividends. Instead, these companies plow all their earnings back into the business. The payoff for shareholders comes from an increase in capital value—the price of their stock— rather than from a stream of income. Mature companies usually pay small dividends in the 2% to 4% range while utilities, which have limited growth potential, pay dividends that can range as high as 6% or 7% of their share value.

The simple way to calculate the yield on a stock is to divide the price of the shares into its annual dividend. For instance, if a stock is trading at $20, and it pays a quarterly dividend of .25, you divide 20 into 1.00 (4 x .25 = $1.00). The quotient is 5, which means that at $20 the shares yield 5%.

Canadian dividends also receive a special tax credit. The purpose of this tax break is to encourage us to buy shares in Canadian companies. However, because it's a tax shelter, the dividend tax credit is irrelevant for shares in an RRSP. On an *after-tax basis*, Canadian dividends are more valuable than interest income. (Dividends are also better, on an after-tax basis, than capital gains.) Tax, however, isn't a consideration in your RRSP. You don't care about net income, you're only concerned with *gross* returns. So, if you want income in your RRSP, the best way to get it is to buy an interest-bearing investment—because equity yields, *on a gross return basis*, are normally lower than medium- to long-term interest yields.

PREFERRED SHARES

Preferred shares are a hybrid security with some of the safety of bonds combined with the dividend tax status of common shares.

Although preferred shares don't normally participate in earnings, and don't have a vote, they are classed as equity (rather than debt) in the company's capitalization. Preferred shares have a par value that must be paid in the event of bankruptcy before any money is paid to the common shareholders. The par value is also used in connection with the dividend rate (i.e., a 7% preferred, if the par value was $25, would pay an annual dividend of $1.75). And preferred dividends—which are a fixed obligation—have a senior claim to earnings over the common shares.

Preferred shares are a defensive type of equity investment. In lieu of capital appreciation, preferreds offer greater safety and higher dividend yields than common shares. This is fine, if you're looking for after-tax income and willing to forfeit growth. But in our RRSP we're looking for gross income. Bonds are not only safer than preferred shares, but they also offer higher yields. *For these reasons, preferred shares—whether they are retractable, floating, or straight preferreds—are unsuitable for a self-directed RRSP.* This applies especially to "straight" preferred shares. Unlike "retractable" preferreds, which you can get out of after a period of time, "straight" preferreds remain outstanding (in theory) forever. This means that if you own a straight preferred and interest rates rise, the price of your shares will fall (just the same as a bond), and you will be locked-in until the cycle changes—which may take years.

Having cautioned you about putting preferred shares into your RRSP, in fairness I should add that there is one exception—convertible preferred shares. Convertible preferred shares are exchangeable into common shares. As well as being convertible, they provide greater safety than the common, and a higher dividend yield. If the price of the underlying common shares goes up, so will the price of your convertible preferred. Should interest rates decline, the preferred will react like a bond and increase in price. And if the worst occurs—interest rates rise and the stock market falls—the convertible preferred, because of its dual nature, will retain its value better than the common or a straight preferred. Later in this chapter we'll look at some of the ways to select a good convertible preferred.

EVALUATING COMMON STOCKS

Now, getting back to equities for your RRSP. Before you make a move, you must differentiate between gambling and investing. Don't confuse low priced mining and oil stocks—the penny dreadfuls—with seasoned blue chip companies. The former are high risk speculations, with the odds heavily stacked against you, while the latter are investments that can provide handsome returns over a long period of time. The cardinal rule is to *stick with quality*—there's no place for junk in your self-directed RRSP. The first step in evaluating a stock is to check the capitalization of the company. The capitalization (or share arrangement) differs from one company to another. Some people think that because "X" company's shares trade at $15 and the shares of company "Y" trade at $20, the shares of company X are cheaper and offer better value. The truth is that it all depends on the capitalization.

Let's say two companies are identical in every respect, and think of them as two pies. One pie is cut into six pieces, the other into twelve pieces. Obviously, although the pies have the same dimensions, the pieces of one pie will be twice as big as the pieces of the other. Now substitute "shares" for pieces, and "company" for "pie." For simplicity we'll say that each company is worth $12,000,000. Company X has six million shares and company Y has twelve million shares. In theory, the shares of company X would be worth twice as much as the shares of company Y. Here's the calculation:

12,000,000 shares divided into $12,000,000 = $1 per share
6,000,000 shares divided into $12,000,000 = $2 per share

When you do this comparison, make sure that you only count "issued" or "outstanding" shares, not the "authorized" shares. Issued or outstanding means the shares are actually in existence (in the hands of the public), while authorized refers to the *maximum* amount of shares that may be issued. It's easy to tell which is which, because it's clearly stated on the balance sheet.

Shares are also designated as having a "par value" in dollars, or "no par value". Par value is the stated face value of a share under the company's charter. In the case of common shares, par value has no connection with market value, and for all practical purposes can be ignored. Indeed, nowadays most companies— even the bluest of the blue chips—designate their common shares as no par value (NPV). The only time par value means something is when it's applied to preferred shares.

Because stock prices are constantly changing, when you analyze a company you'll need to work with the most recent figures. One of the best sources of current information is the business section of your newspaper. *The Financial Post* and *The Globe & Mail* are the two most comprehensive dailies, but any major newspaper will give you plenty of financial data to chew on. Here's a typical newspaper stock quotation:

ROYAL BANK STOCK QUOTE

| Price Range for Past Year | Company | Stock Symbol | Trading Range for the day | | Price Change on the Day | Trading Volume | Closing Price Yield |

| 52-week | | | | | | Vol | | P/E |
| high | low | Stock | Sym | Div | High | Low | Close | Chg | (100s) | Yield | Ratio |

S-T

| 31¼ | 25⅞ | Royal Bank | RY | 1.24 | 29⅞ | 29½ | 29½ | | 20552 | 4.20 | 8.6 |

Annual Dividend

Closing Price - Price/Earnings Ratio

This single line of numbers contains a surprising amount of information. Most of the entries are self-explanatory, except for the Price/Earnings Ratio. Because this is a closely watched figure it's an important financial yardstick. To calculate the price/earnings ratio, you must refer to the capitalization and find out how many common shares are outstanding. Then you divide the number of common shares into the company's net earnings. This gives you another significant piece of information—the earnings per share. To get the P/E ratio you divide the earnings per share into the market price of the stock. Let's say, for example, that a company has 4,000,000 shares outstanding and net earnings of $6,000,000. This works out to $1.50 per share. If the market value of the common shares is $15, and you divide this price by $1.50 (the EPS) you come up with a P/E ratio of 10:1. As an aside, it's common practice for the financial industry and the press to leave off the 1 in ratios, and simply use the quotient (which in this case is 10).

A price/earnings ratio will tell you at a glance three things:

- The first is how cheap or expensive the stock is in relation to its earnings.
- The second is how cheap or expensive the stock is *in relation to other companies in the same industry.*
- And the third is how cheap or expensive the stock is in relation to the general market.

Because P/E ratioes differ with each industry and the stage of the economic cycle, there's no absolute figure or magic number that will tell you when to buy or sell. And you can't generalize and assume that because the average price/earnings ratio on the TSE is 16, that a stock selling at a P/E of 14 is a bargain. Where price/earnings ratios are most useful is in measuring *relative* values. This applies particularily to industry groups—such as the banks and the utilities—that trade on a similar P/E basis. Groups that differ widely in their ratios—like industrial product companies, are much more difficult to compare.

As I write this, I'm thinking of buying shares in the Bank of Montreal. Before me is a research bulletin on the chartered banks. I see that the Bank of Montreal's P/E ratio is 9.7x, and the *average* P/E ratio of all the major banks is 10.3x. Based strictly on its P/E ratio (and there are other measurements to take into consideration), Bank of Montreal shares appear cheaper than its competitors. The next thing I'm going to check is the *book value per share.*

Book value per share tells you the amount of assets behind each common share, and is sometimes referred to as the "price to book." To find the BV you deduct the company's debts (plus the par value of any preferred shares) from its total assets. Then you divide the balance by the number of outstanding common shares. Here's a sample book value calculation:

Company's total assets	$21,000,000
less total debt	–$11,000,000
sub total	$10,000,000
less par value of preferred	–$ 3,000,000
net balance	$ 7,000,000
number of common shares	1,000,000
divided into $7,000,000 =	$7

Book value has to be interpreted with some judgement because it can be misleading. One obvious flaw is that the assets can be understated or overstated. For instance, a company might have real estate holdings that have appreciated but are shown at an unrealistically low value. Conversely, a manufacturer or merchandiser might have outdated inventory or stock that is shown at an unrealistically high price. Even if the valuation is correct, are the assets *marketable* at that price? And supposing they are marketable, what would the chance be of the company liquidating all its assets? Book value also varies with the type of business, and its stage of development. Relatively speaking, service companies have much lower book values than capital goods and resource industries. The same is true of young growth companies compared to mature companies.

All this might suggest that book value isn't worth looking at. In fact, it's a valuable tool for establishing *relative* values. *This is particularly true when comparing the banks or utility stocks.* And variations on the book value theme—such as ounces of gold per share or barrels of oil per share—are also useful in ferreting out "best buys" in the resource industries.

When you assess a stock you should focus your sights on the future, not what's happening today. Smart investors buy on the basis of earnings six to nine months from now—and so should you. Depending on the stage of the economy, failing to look beyond the end of your nose can lead to nasty surprises. For instance, a parts manufacturer is making bags of money and the stock is hitting new highs. You buy the shares on the strength of current earnings. Unfortunately, it's late in the cycle, and it's the final stage of the auto boom. Six months later, car sales dwindle, and the stock plunges. If you'd looked ahead—instead of concentrating on the present—you could have avoided serious loss. Yet, even this scenario has a silver lining, if you look ahead. After car sales have been flat for some months you buy more shares in the parts manufacturer. By this time earnings have fallen off, the stock is cheap, and nobody is recommending it. Although the current situation is lousy you ignore the company's present results, because you know that eventually auto sales are bound to pick up. When this happens, earnings of the parts manufacturer will improve and, inevitably, so will the price of the shares.

STRATEGIES FOR BUILDING A STOCK PORTFOLIO IN YOUR RRSP

In broad terms there are two types of common shares—those that are bought strictly for capital gain, and those that provide a combination of growth and income. Within these broad categories, there are a number of sub-groups. But before we look at them, let's review the grading system for common stocks. At the top of the list we have the "blue chips." These are well established companies with consistent earnings and a long history of paying dividends. Some of the names that come to mind are: BCE, Trans-Canada Pipeline, Canadian Pacific, Molson, Imperial Oil, and the senior chartered banks. The next tier (where some of the best capital gains are made) consists of companies with less consistent earnings: recovering businesses that have turned around their earnings, and major emerging companies. Below this group, you have a raft of "small cap" stocks: companies with small capitalizations that are in the early stages of growth. Small cap stocks are relatively high risk, but produce some of the most spectacular gains (usually late in the business cycle). At the bottom of the pile are the "spec" stocks that have little in the way of assets, but are kept in play by hype. Needless to say, speculative stocks are very dangerous, and the risks far exceed the potential rewards.

Blue chip stocks, and the tier below them, are suitable for your RRSP. There's also a place for small cap stocks, but because of the risk factor, I would buy a "package" of them through a good mutual fund. Don't—no matter how persuasive the story—buy spec stocks for your RRSP. If you must take a flutter, do it with funds outside your retirement plan.

Growth Stocks

The most obvious growth stocks are found in the "sunrise industries"—telecommunication companies, computer manufacturers, software producers, cable companies and the like. These companies typically sell at high P/E ratios, pay little or no dividends, and fluctuate dramatically in price. High-tech stocks often perform like high speed elevators, shooting up with breathtaking speed on good news, and plummeting on bad. If you know something about the high-tech world (or have a good advisor) you can make a lot of money in the sunrise industries. But you need a strong stomach.

Cyclical Stocks

Cyclical companies can also be growth stocks—if you buy them at the right stage of the economic cycle. Cyclical industries are especially sensitive to the general economy or to changes in the price of commodities. They include steel makers, parts suppliers, mining companies, oil and gas companies, cement producers, and the forest products industry. They aren't as glamorous as the high-tech stocks, but if your timing is right they can produce huge gains. The trick with cyclical stocks is to buy them when they're out of favour—when they're stock market pariahs—and to sell them when everybody says they're going through the roof. This strategy requires discipline, patience, and a certain amount of courage, but can be extremely rewarding.

Debt leverage is an advantage in a cyclical stock. If a company has a lot of debt, it accentuates the earnings and price swings. The cost of servicing bond debt is a fixed charge which, in tough times, can leave nothing for the common shares. The reverse is true in good times—once you've paid the bond interest, all the rest goes to the shareholders. For example let's say it costs a company $1,000,000 to pay its annual bond interest. If it can earn $1,200,000, there will be $200,000 left over (before taxes) for the shareholders. However, should the earnings fall short by only 15% this is what happens:

Actual earnings	$1,020,000
Cost to service debt	–$1,000,000
Available for common shares	$20,000

This shows the downside of a heavily debt leveraged company. Now let's see what a 15% *increase* in earning will do for the common shares:

Actual earnings	$1,380,000
Cost to service debt	–$1,000,000
Available for common shares	$380,000

Note that a 15% increase has nearly doubled the pre-tax amount available for the common shareholders. That's debt leverage. If you buy a cyclical stock at the end of a recession, or early in the recovery, you'll be amazed at the rebound in earnings. But don't get mesmerized by the dazzling numbers each successive quarter. Cyclical stocks reach a crest, and then it's another long slide downhill. So remember to sell them.

Gold Shares

Gold shares are "closet" cyclicals because gold is a commodity. Gold stocks also fit into the growth category, if only because they pay little or no dividends. Whether or not you should invest in gold for your RRSP remains to be seen. I suppose it depends on your attitude towards the metal. Some people—known as "goldbugs"—are fascinated by gold and feel compelled to own it. You can't hold bullion or coins in your RRSP, but you can hold gold mining shares and mutual funds.

Gold is a rare and precious element. It is used extensively for jewellery, and also has industrial applications. Its main role, however, is as a storehouse of wealth. Unlike paper money, gold needs no one's signature to make it valuable. And it is used to back—to a small degree—some of the world's major currencies. Gold is a popular inflation hedge because it has retained its purchasing power through the centuries. Historians tell us that the same amount of gold will buy the same amount of wheat that it bought three hundred years ago. The same, obviously, can't be said for paper currencies.

So much for the intrinsic value of gold. In recent years, gold mining shares (paper) have outperformed bullion by a wide margin. In this connection, there's a huge selection of gold mining stocks to choose from in Canada. These companies range from investment grade giants to drill hole gambles. If you're going to invest in gold you should restrict yourself to mines that meet the following criteria:

1. Substantial proven reserves

2. Low production cost

3. Favourable political/environmental location

4. Good management

5. Strong balance sheet

Ore reserves determine the life span of a mine. You want *proven* reserves not "estimated" or "probable" reserves. The production cost is critical to the mine's profitability. If the cost of production is high, say $350 per ounce, then the mine will be a marginal producer and have little latitude with the price of gold. Should the world price fall below $350 per ounce, the mine will have to cease production or operate at a loss. A favourable political location means that the mine should be located in a stable part of the world, preferably North America. (This may sound xenophobic, but in the event of a political coup, nasty things can happen to foreign businesses in banana republics.) Assuming that the mine is in North America, environmental risks should be checked out before you buy the shares. Good management and a strong balance sheet are basic requisites, and apply to virtually any equity investment.

It might be helpful if I winnow through the list of Canadian gold mining companies and mention a few that I think are suitable for an RRSP. All these stocks are listed on the TSE, and several are also listed in New York and on other exchanges. But a word of warning, share prices of these mining companies are tied to the price of gold, and nobody (including the goldbugs) can predict what the future price will be. Here are the names, in alphabetical order:

Agnico-Eagle Mines	Newmont Gold
Barrick Gold Corp.	Placer Dome
Franco-Nevada Mining	Teck Corporation
Glamis Gold	TVX Gold

This is by no means a definitive list, and because of mergers and new discoveries, the situation within the gold mining industry is constantly changing. But these names will give you something to start with. If you prefer an even more conservative way to play the golds, you might buy one of the closed or open-ended mutual funds that specialize in gold and precious metals (these are discussed in the "Mutual Funds" chapter).

I think we tend to exaggerate the importance of gold stocks in this country. There are, however, a number of understandable reasons for our skewed perspective. The first is that Canada is a major gold producer—the third largest in the world. And because we have so many gold mines, there are a disproportionate number of gold stocks listed on the TSE. Brokers like to tout gold stocks because they generate commissions, and their customers like to buy them because they're exciting speculative vehicles. Gold is also buoyed by propaganda. No matter what its price, we are constantly told by zealous goldbugs that gold is the key to our financial salvation. Finally, gold symbolizes wealth, it is rare, and for many it has a visceral appeal.

Which brings us back to the question: should you buy gold shares for your RRSP? Gold is considered the ultimate refuge in the event of war or a currency collapse, and a sovereign hedge against inflation. Yet when the Gulf War began, the price of gold, instead of rising, fell dramatically. It's also worth noting that the price of gold in January of 1980, was $800 an ounce. Fifteen years later, in January of 1995, the price was less than $400 an ounce. Not much of an inflation hedge, at least over the short term. And, when gold shares are in the doldrums—as they have been for long periods in the past—they offer little or no compensating income. My conclusion, after years in the investment business, is that investors lose more often than they win with gold stocks. So, unless you're a dyed-in-the-wool goldbug, I would suggest there are better ways to hedge against inflation in your RRSP.

Energy and Base Metal Stocks

Energy and base metal stocks are better investments for your RRSP than gold stocks. Unlike gold, which is constantly being recycled (your wedding band may have started out as part of a goblet owned by a Spanish grandee), fuels and metals are consumed. This means that they must be replaced, and ensures an ongoing demand. Canada is richly endowed with base metal mines as well as oil and gas reserves. Thus, there's no shortage of these stocks to buy for your RRSP.

First, let's look at the mines. Like our gold producers, Canadian base metal mines range from multinational conglomerates to small speculative promotions. Virtually all the major mines are listed on the Toronto Stock Exchange. The Vancouver Stock Exchange also has many listings, but most of them are low-priced stocks that bring to mind the tongue-in-cheek definition of a mine as "a hole in the ground with a liar standing at the top." Because metal prices fluctuate with the world economy, producing mines have cyclical earnings. From your standpoint, this means you can't simply buy them and forget them. You should keep an eye on the state of the economy—whether it's gathering steam, or entering a recession—as well as price trends in the metal your mine produces (i.e., if you held Inco shares, you'd want to know the outlook for nickel).

Huge profits are made by investors who spot a major mining discovery early in the game, and ride the shares to dizzying heights. For those of you with with the foresight (or luck) to pick winners like this, I have nothing but envy. However, no matter how big the payoff this is still gambling, not investing—and you don't want to gamble with your retirement funds. For this reason, I would strongly suggest you avoid mines that are still in the drilling stage. Instead, put your money into proven orebodies that are already in production. This way you'll eliminate the greatest risk in mining—that of not finding a commercial orebody. If you take this conservative tack, and you play the mining cycle, you can still make very good money.

The mining cycle can be broken down into three phases, each of which ends with a pullback. The first or "anticipation" phase, lifts the price of the metal and the shares of the senior producers from the doldrums. This typically occurs at the end of a recession. At this stage, there's only a flicker of demand for the metal and the mines are making little, if any, money. At the conclusion of this phase stocks give up some of their gains—usually from a quarter to a half—and it's easy to write the move off as a false start. In fact, it's a golden opportunity to buy because the cycle has started, stocks are still cheap, and the best is yet to come. The next upward leg, known as the "fundamental phase" is driven by higher metal prices and dramatically higher earnings. Again, there's a pullback at the end of this phase. The final and most sensational move is the "speculative phase," which is powered by panic buying of the metal and record earnings by the mines. This period of euphoria is the time to sell your shares. Prices eventually peak and, after churning back and forth without moving higher, start their downward slide. The cycle is over. Here's what the mining cycle looks like in a simple graph:

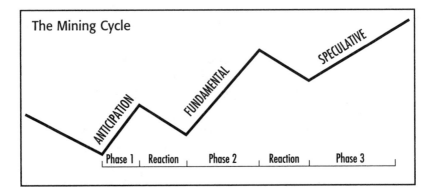

Choosing a metal to invest in is not too difficult. Your broker can advise you, and provide research material on the prospects for the main base metals. If the demand for aluminum is strong, and supplies are tight, you might choose an aluminum stock. A bullish outlook for car sales means increased consumption of lead and zinc (lead is used in car batteries and zinc for galvanizing). An active construction industry consumes large amounts of copper, aluminum, and steel as well as lumber. The demand for nickel and molybdenum is tied to the steel industry, which uses both elements to make alloys.

Once you've chosen a particular metal, your next step is to check out the mines that are primary producers. (Most major mining companies produce a range of metals, some of which are by-products of the recovery process.) Crunch the numbers and do your homework the same as you would with any other stock. To find the best relative value, compare price/earnings ratios, book values, costs of production, and production per share. When you compare ore grades (the amount of metal per ton of ore) be sure to take into account the type of mine. Open pit mines can get by with much lower grades of ore than shaft mines, because it's cheaper to extract ore from an open pit. Canadian mines export a high percentage of their production, so currency values also enter the picture. A one cent move in the Canadian dollar in relation to the U.S. dollar—in either direction—can dramatically affect a mine's earnings.

Senior mining companies, in mid-cycle, usually trade at around 10 times earnings and yield from zero to 4 percent. Investors accept low dividends because they don't buy mining shares for income, but for the ore in the ground (as an inflation hedge). If you spot a mine with a high yield, you can be sure that something is wrong. The most likely reason for the high yield is that the mine is running out of ore. In this case the outsize dividend represents a return of capital. Eventually, there'll be nothing left. As a *minimum*, you want a mine with at least five years of reserves, and preferably two or three times that much.

Oil and gas stocks are another excellent inflation hedge. Because energy is a necessity, oil and gas prices move in tandem with the rate of inflation. (If you doubt this, think of how the price of gas for your car, or oil for your furnace, has increased in the last ten years.) Canada is fortunate to have sizeable reserves of both oil and gas. Most of the country's oil is found in Alberta, while our main natural gas reserves are located in the Prairie provinces. In the near future it's likely that significant amounts of natural gas will be produced off Nova Scotia, and there are also untapped oil reserves off Newfoundland.

Canada has a surplus of natural gas, and exports billions of cubic feet to the States under long-term contracts. So much natural gas has been discovered in the Canadian West that many of the wells are capped. Over the near term, this surplus tends to depress export prices. But consumption of natural gas in the U.S. exceeds the discovery of new reserves, so it's only a matter of time before a shortage of supply pulls prices higher. For this reason, a capped natural gas well is money in the bank.

The oil picture is not as rosy. Canada is an importer of oil, particularily in the East. To add to the problem, oil is more difficult and more expensive to find than natural gas. The importance of oil is underlined by the fact that its price is the benchmark for all energy prices. Oil prices are determined by the state of the world economy and, to a lesser extent, by the machinations of OPEC (OPEC stands for the Organization of Petroleum Exporting Countries). In the seventies, OPEC reefed oil prices to alarming heights, and held the rest of the world hostage. Since then, however, chicanery and cheating among its members have greatly reduced the effectiveness of the cartel.

The current or "spot" world oil price is expressed in U.S. dollars, and is based on the price of West Texas Intermediate Crude (WTI). Sometimes you'll see a second oil price quoted—Brent Crude. Brent refers to the price of oil from the North Sea, and is of less significance than West Texas Intermediate. My reason for dwelling on the world oil price is that both *oil and natural gas shares move up and down in lock step with it.* Here's a graph covering a four-month period that shows the direct link between the price of oil and the Toronto Stock Exchange Oil and Gas Index.

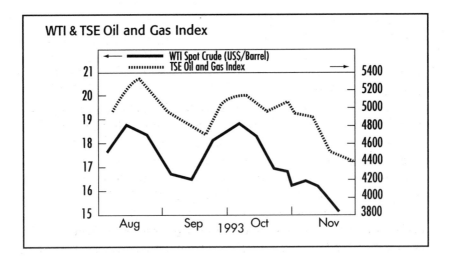

Canadian oil and gas companies fall into two basic cate- gories. Integrated oils are the big guys who do everything from exploring for oil to selling the refined products at their own ser- vice stations. Imperial Oil, Petro-Canada, Shell, and Suncor are among the best known integrated oils. If you research the inte- grated companies you'll likely encounter references to their "upstream" and "downstream" earnings. Upstream refers to their operations before the oil gets to the refinery; downstream refers to their operations after the oil has been refined. Companies that aren't integrated make up the second category, and are simply known as "producers." Producers usually sell their oil in the crude state, before it gets to the refinery. Most producers have both oil and gas interests, although some concentrate exclusive- ly on one or the other. Producing companies are ranked by stock analysts as being senior, intermediate, or junior producers. On a risk basis (next to the integrated oils), the senior producers are the safest, while the junior exploration companies are the most dangerous—and potentially the most rewarding. Canadian Occidental, Poco Petroleum and Renaissance Energy are familiar names in the long list of producing companies.

There are only five integrated oils to choose from, but dozens of exploration and production companies. What should you look for when buying these stocks? Integrated oils are assessed much the same way as industrial stocks—by taking into account profit margins, book values, price/earnings ratios, and comparative yields, as well as their oil and gas reserves. Producers are mea- sured a little differently, because often they have no earnings, and their book values can be suspect. Instead, when you look at producing and exploration companies the most meaningful fig- ure is their cash flow.

Cash flow is the sum of net income plus deferred taxes plus noncash charges, such as amortization, depreciation, and deple- tion. (Depreciation is an allowance for obsolescence as well as wear and tear on buildings and equipment, while depletion is an allowance for the removal of a resource.) The cash flow figure tells you how much is available for exploration, and is expressed as a ratio to the stock price. Every company is different, but a P/CF ratio of 3x to 5x is reasonable for producers. Integrated companies trade on a combination of figures which include price/earnings, book value, and yield. A reasonable valuation for an integrated oil in mid-cycle would be a P/E of 12 to 16, a price to book of 1 to 1.25 and a yield of around 3 percent.

If you're comparing two companies, and one has all its properties in North America, and the other has exposure overseas, pick the one with its assets on this continent (preferably in Canada and the U.S.). Resource stocks have enough variables without throwing in political and war risks. An example of a political risk is the overthrow of the government, and confiscation of your assets by the new regime. An example of war risk is a conflict in your area in which your oil wells are torched, or your pipeline is blown up. By sticking with domestic producers, you can avoid these offshore dangers.

Utility Stocks

Utility stocks are another consideration for your RRSP. They are the plowhorses of the investment stable, and plod along without regard to the economic cycle. Indeed, being non-cyclical is one of their virtues. When the economy is flat and most stocks are in the doldrums, the utilities continue to make good money because of the constant need for light, heat, and power.

Utility stocks—such as BCE Inc., Nova Scotia Power, Consumers Gas, and Telus—pay out a relatively high proportion of their earnings, and are usually bought for their income. Being interest sensitive, *they thrive when interest rates are declining or at a low level.* For this reason, they're excellent investments during a recession. The best time to buy utility shares (or pipelines, which are similar) is when interest rates are peaking, or have reached the double digits. This usually occurs in the last phase of the economic cycle.

I said earlier that if you want income in your RRSP, bonds are better than stocks. This is true. But if you want a good low risk total return, utility stocks are hard to beat. By total return I mean a blend of dividend income and capital appreciation. For instance, if you bought a utility stock for $20 with a yield of 6%, and the stock advanced just $2.00 over the course of the year, your total return would be a very respectable 16% (6% dividend + 10% capital gain).

Bank Stocks

The chartered banks can also provide consistent total returns for your RRSP. The banks have a wonderful franchise, and providing they don't get carried away by greed (which they have done on several occasions) they're a superb investment. A chartered bank operates similar to a casino in that every time someone plays, the bank takes a piece of the action. And as far as safety goes, if the chartered banks fail, the fate of your other securities will be academic. The big five (Bank of Montreal, CIBC, Nova Scotia, TD, and Royal) are attractive buys whenever their price/earnings ratios are in the 7x to 9x range, and their yields exceed 4 percent. If you're not sure which one to buy, pick the bank you deal with. This will take some of the sting out of those service charges— and no matter which one you choose, you can hardly go wrong.

Convertible Preferred Shares

Convertible preferred shares can provide the best of both worlds—growth and income. But you have to choose carefully. As mentioned earlier, convertible preferreds can be exchanged at a stated rate for the company's common shares. Because of their dual nature, convertible preferred yields are normally lower than "straight" preferred shares, and the conversion rate is usually higher than the current market price. Let me give you a hypothetical example. If straight preferred yields are around 7% and the market price of the common stock is $15, a convertible preferred might yield 6% and be exchangeable for the common at a price of $20 per share. The difference between the conversion price and the market price is known as the "time premium," (in this case 33%). A time premium is to be expected with most convertible preferred shares.

Indeed, if you see a convertible preferred trading at a discount with little or no premium, something is amiss—either the outlook for the company is lousy, or the shares are vulnerable to being called at any time. You should also be wary if a convertible trades at a big premium, because you don't want to pay too much for it. To determine whether the premium is reasonable you have to calculate the "payback period" (how long it will take for the dividends to pay off the premium). And, if it's callable, you should also check the redemption terms. Let's take the example of a convertible preferred I just used, and assume that the common pays no dividend. Here's how you work out the payback period.

convertible preferred yield	6%
less common yield	nil
additional preferred yield	6%
divide yield difference of 6% into 33% premium	
payback period =	5.5 years

After finding the payback period, we then look up the redemption terms of the preferred. If the issue is callable in less than five-and-a-half years, the conservative strategy is not to buy it (because it could be called before the payback is completed). However, if the company has dynamic potential, and you've got at least three years for the common shares to make their move, I might take a calculated risk and buy the preferred. This brings us to a fundamental reason for choosing a convertible preferred share—because you like the prospects for the company. If you aren't bullish about the common stock, don't buy the convertible.

The other thing you should watch for is the expiration of the conversion feature. Some convertibles become straight preferred shares on a given date, or the conversion rate changes to a higher (and less attractive) price. The good news is that when a convertible preferred is redeemed, you will always have the opportunity to convert into common shares before the call date. For instance, you might own a convertible preferred that is called at $26 when the intrinsic value is $28, and (because of the time premium) the preferred stock is trading at $30. Instead of accepting the redemption price of $26, you can convert into the common and sell your shares for the equivalent of $28. This is less than the market price of the preferred before it was called, but considerably more than the redemption price.

Stock Splits

From time to time, companies split their common shares. When this happens each share you presently hold is "split" or subdivided into new shares. Terms of share splits differ, but the effect is the same. If you hold 100 shares and they're split 2 for 1, you end up with 200 shares; if they're split 3 for 1 you will have 300 shares, and so on. *When a stock is split you don't get any more of the pie, just smaller pieces.* Companies split their stock to lower its price and thus make the shares more affordable to the investing public. For instance, if a company's shares are trading at $45, and they are split 3 for 1, the "new" shares will have a theoretical price of $15 (45 divided by 3 = 15). Although no intrinsic value is added, newly split shares often trade above their theoretical value, sometimes by a quarter or a half a dollar. For this reason share splits tend to increase the total value of a holding, and are welcomed by investors.

Split Shares

At the risk of confusing you, in addition to share splits there are also *split shares.* Split shares are a derivative security in which the dividend income and the capital growth of a stock are split into two portions and marketed separately. The income portion receives *all* the dividends, and is in effect a "synthetic preferred," while the growth portion functions much like a stock purchase warrant. Split shares have both a formal name and an acronym. The dividend portion is called a Payment Enhanced Capital Security (PEAC), while the growth portion is called a Special Equity Claim Security (SPEC). I have yet to meet anyone in the business who calls them by their formal name, or for that matter, by their acronym.

Split shares are usually created by a broker or a syndicate of brokers, who buy a large block of stock on the exchange. Bank and utility stocks are favourites because they embody growth and stability, and they pay good dividends. The shares are then arbitrarily split into income and growth components, and a date is set for the components to be redeemed. The "preferred share" portion is assigned a par value which will be paid (market permitting) on the redemption date. In the meantime, the preferred will receive all the dividends, including any increases. The "capital share" portion receives the value of the underlying stock, including any appreciation, on the redemption date, *less the par value of the preferred shares*. Split shares may be more easily understood if you think of Jack Sprat and his wife—one gets all the income, the other gets all the capital gain.

Split preferred shares carry some risk because, at redemption, their par value is paid by the underlying shares. If the market value of the underlying stock falls below the par value, the preferred shareholders bear the loss. In practice, the risk is negligible. Not only are the underlying shares defensive in nature, but the par value is a small percentage of the underlying stock price. The difference between the par value and the stock price provides a substantial cushion. Take for example, the split shares of Telus (the Alberta telephone company). Telus preferred shares have a par value of $10.50, and the capital growth shares have an exercise price of $10.50. Both shares are redeemable/retractable 31 July 1998. Here are the numbers on Telus split shares when the underlying common shares were trading at $16.625 in the summer of 1995.

PREFERRED SHARES

dividend	market price	retraction price	current yield	downside protection
.81	$11.375	$10.50	7.04%	36.84%

You'll notice that the market price is higher than the redemption price. This means that buyers will lose seven-eighths of a point (.875) when the shares are redeemed in 1998. However, because of the current level of interest rates, buyers are prepared to take this loss, and amortize it over the remaining term. The other point worth noting is the downside protection. Telus shares will have to fall more than 36% before there's any reduction to the par value of the preferred. On balance, the preferred shares appear reasonably safe. Now let's take a look at the capital shares:

CAPITAL SHARES

price of common	price of cap share	exercise price	discount	leverage
$16.625	$5.25	$10.50	5.26%	3.17X

As you can see, the capital shares are trading at a discount of $.875 from their break-up value of $6.125 ($16.625—$10.50 = $6.125). This is not unusual, and occurs because of the time delay to the redemption date. Normally, as the redemption date approaches, the discount will decline and eventually disappear. Leverage—which is the main appeal of capital shares—is also clearly shown. At these prices a move in Telus will be magnified 3.17 times by the capital shares. However, as well as the upside potential, there's also the downside to consider. In this connection, capital shares can lose all their value if the underlying stock falls below the exercise price. This suggests (at least in theory) that they carry substantial risk. However, because the underlying shares are usually blue chips, in practice the risk is minimal.

Should you have split shares in your RRSP? I wouldn't buy the preferred shares because their gross yields are no better than bonds, and their par value isn't guaranteed on redemption. But I *would* consider capital shares, especially those of the banks, and there are a number of interesting issues to choose from.

Stock Options

Stock options are another derivative that you can use in your self-directed RRSP. (A "derivative" is a security derived from another type of security.) An option gives you the right to buy or sell something at a fixed price, for a given period of time. Options are often used in the real estate business. For instance, if a person is interested in buying a property he might offer the owner a sum of money for the right to buy the property at a specific price until a certain date.

The same principle applies to stock options. Although options have been around for centuries, stock options have only been traded in Canada for the past twenty years. And not all listed stocks have options—only the largest and most actively traded companies.

There are two types of stock options: "call" options and "put" options. A call option gives you the right to buy a certain number of shares at a fixed price for a fixed period of time *regardless of the market price*. A put option is the reverse. A put option allows you to *sell* shares on the same basis.

Options are highly leveraged; not only do they cost a fraction of the underlying stock, but a single call or put represents the right to buy or sell 100 shares. The price at which the option may be exercised is known as the *strike price* or the *exercise price*. This is described simply by a number, for example 25. The term of the option is identified by the month (and sometimes the year) in which it expires. Options normally trade in nine-month cycles, and expire on the third Friday of the final month. The price of a stock option is called the premium. The premium consists of intrinsic value and time value. Intrinsic value is its actual value based on the market price of the underlying shares. Time value is the value attributed to the period remaining before the option expires. If the shares underlying a call option are below the strike price, the option has no intrinsic value (but it may have time value). If the shares are above the strike price, the option may have *both* intrinsic and time value. Let's suppose that a call option has a strike price of $25. The underlying shares are trading at $26, and the market price of the calls is $3. Here's how you calculate the values:

```
market price of underlying shares    $26
strike price of calls                -$25

intrinsic value of option             $1
option cost less intrinsic value ($3–$1) = $2 time value
```

As well as buying call options in the hope that they will increase in value, you can also *sell* call options. When you sell (or "write" as it's termed in the trade) a call option, *you give the buyer the right to buy your shares at a fixed price*. In return, you receive all the premium. Once you've sold the calls the buyer can force you at any time until the expiry date to sell him your shares at the strike price, regardless of the current market price. If, however, the shares are below the strike price when the option expires, the options will be worthless. In this happy circumstance, you pocket the premium *and* keep your shares.

Selling call options on shares that you own is called "covered writing." Selling calls on shares that you don't own is called "naked" writing. You may buy call options or write covered options, but these are the *only* type of option transactions permitted in your RRSP. All the other types of option trades are considered too risky for a retirement plan. And, before you can write any call options, you must fill in two special forms.

Buying call options in the hope that they will increase in value is a high risk/high reward game. It's also easy to understand because if the underlying stock goes up, so will the calls. You get tremendous leverage, and fast action—sometimes too fast. Let's take for example a bluechip industrial stock trading at $40. A thousand shares will cost you $40,000, but ten calls at $3 will cost only $3000. If the strike price is 40, and the shares increase by 10%, this is what happens:

cost of 1000 shares at $40 $40,000
cost of 10 calls @ $3 $ 3000

price of shares rise 10% to $44
1000 shares now worth $44,000
10 calls now worth $4000
profit on shares $4000 or 10%
profit on calls $1000 or 33⅓%

In this example I've not given the calls any time value, just their intrinsic value. Even so, the leverage is dramatic. I should also warn you that because most options have a maximum life span of nine months, they often expire worthless. *Should this happen, you will lose your entire investment.* A more conservative strategy is to buy calls to lock in the cost of shares you intend to buy in the future. This is particularily appropriate for growth stocks, because they can rise sharply in a short period of time.

Covered writing, if you're a highly sophisticated investor, can increase the return on your portfolio. The trick is to sell calls on stocks that aren't going anywhere—ones that will expire worthless. This of course begs the question why you would want to hold this type of stock in the first place. Then again, it might be a good stock, but you feel the whole market is about to fall—in which case you'll have made the right move. Or, if one of your stocks has had a good run, and you're concerned it might slip back, you could write calls. Should the stock continue up, and you subsequently lose it, you'll have sold the shares for the strike price *plus* the premium. (If the strike price is $35 and you sell the calls for $3.50, the effective sale price would be $35 + $3.50 or $38.50 per share.)

Whatever the reason, try to get as big a premium as you can for as short a term as possible. This isn't easy, because the longer the term, the greater an option's time value. A useful rule of thumb is to only write calls if you can get a premium equal to at least 10% of the value of the underlying shares (i.e., if your shares are trading at $25, you want a minimum premium of $2.50).

Should you buy calls for your RRSP? Only if you intend to buy the underlying shares, otherwise it's too risky. What about writing covered call options on stocks in your RRSP? I wouldn't do that either. In my opinion, it's a mug's game. The chances are that your broker will be the only one who'll make any money.

Initial Public Offerings (IPOs)

New issues of common shares (called initial public offerings or IPOs) are sold to the public from time to time—usually when there's a lot of optimism in the air and the stock market is moving into new high ground. Each issue has to be judged *carefully*, especially offerings of "high-tech" stocks with no previous track record. Some people buy new issues hoping to make a quick buck. They have no intention of holding the security, but plan to be in and out before the payment date. These people are known as "riders" in the investment business, and this practice is frowned upon (because after the rider dumps the security, the underwriter has to sell it again or take it into inventory). The scarcity of a new offering determines how "hot" it will be—the scarcer the issue, the more likely it will trade at a premium. Conversely, if there's strong sales pressure on you to buy an IPO, the greater the likelihood it will end up in the tank. *Riding new issues has no place in the management of a self-directed RRSP.*

Rights and Warrants

Rights to purchase common shares (rather than the common shares themselves) are another security eligible for your self-directed RRSP. Companies issue "rights" to raise more capital, and at the same time to protect the equity of existing shareholders. A right allows the holder to purchase an additional share (or a portion of one) at a discount from the current market price. Normally, for each share that you hold, you'll receive one right. Rights can be exercised, or sold on the market. Either way they have value, and are a benefit to shareholders.

Purchase terms of rights offerings vary from issue to issue. But the formula is always X many rights *plus* X amount of cash buys one new share. For example, if the shares of a company are trading at $30, it might take 5 rights plus $25 to buy one new share. In this example each right would have a *theoretical* value of $1. Here's the simple equation:

5 rights + $25 = $30 (one share)
5 rights = $30–$25
5 rights = $5
1 right = $1

Because chartered banks and utilities like to issue rights, and these stocks are often owned in RRSPs, you may be faced with a decision on a rights issue. Basically you can't lose, but there are a couple of things to keep in mind. The first is that rights expire, and if you don't do something about them promptly, they'll be worthless. The other thing to remember is you can exercise them (buy more shares) only if you have sufficient contribution room—and the cash—in your RRSP. If you don't have the cash, or sufficient contribution room, you simply sell the rights.

A rights issue usually expires in four to eight weeks. However, there are also long-term rights, called "warrants," with terms of several years. Except for the time period, warrants are identical to rights. Unless you're keen on a company that has warrants, and want to use their leverage to speculate on the stock, there's not much sense (and considerable risk) in buying warrants for your RRSP.

Secondary Offerings

As well as rights issues on existing shares, there are also "secondary offerings" of shares. A secondary offering occurs when a block of stock is to be sold, but it's too large to be absorbed in normal trading on the exchange. The sale is made by offering the shares (through a syndicate of brokers) to investors at a discount from the closing market price. Often there's no warning of a secondary, and it lasts only a matter of hours. Because speed is essential, when your broker phones he may press you for an immediate answer. Don't be stampeded into a rash decision. Unless you have had your eye on that particular stock, the few pennies discount rarely justifies buying it.

I don't like "quickie" secondary offerings because you don't have time to do your homework. But secondary offerings accompanied by a prospectus are another matter. (A prospectus provides comprehensive information on a forthcoming issue.) My favourite secondary offerings are those that market the stock through share receipts. A share receipt allows you to buy on a time payment plan. You start off by paying for only part of a share, but you get the full dividend. This provides great leverage, and a very generous yield. Terms differ, but a typical share receipt issue will require roughly 40% down, and the balance—usually in two instalments—over eighteen months.

Providing you're bullish on the the shares—not just dazzled by the yield on the first instalment—it's worth buying this type of investment. Indeed, share receipts are often outstanding market performers. But keep in mind that a share receipt is only a down-payment, and further payments will be required. So you'll have to calculate your future cashflow *and* your contribution room, before you buy one for your RRSP. Should it turn out that you don't have the money or the room, you can of course sell the receipts before the second instalment is due.

But that would turn the investment into a short-term speculation, and it's not smart to speculate with your retirement savings plan. Over the long haul, a conservative approach will pay off. Especially with equities.

8

Mutual Funds

A mutual fund is an ideal investment for a self-directed retirement plan. And the good news is that there are plenty of funds to choose from. More than 700 are sold in Canada, encompassing everything from money market securities to Third World growth stocks. If you want, it's perfectly feasible to invest solely in mutual funds for your RRSP.

What is a mutual fund? A mutual fund is a company or trust whose assets consist of cash and securities. The fund is professionally managed for its shareholders. Mutual fund shares—which are also known as "units"—represent a percentage of the total portfolio. The price of these shares or units rises and falls with fluctuations in the value of the fund's investments. The amount you get when you cash in mutual fund shares (except for some money market and a few segregated funds) is *not* guaranteed.

There are, in fact, two types of mutual funds: "open-end" and "closed-end." Open-end funds are by far the most common, and the most appropriate for an RRSP. The main difference between an open-end fund and a closed-end fund is that an open-end fund buys back (redeems) its shares, and a closed-end fund does not.

Closed-end funds, also called investment trusts, have a fixed number of shares and are traded over-the-counter or on a stock exchange. Although their assets consist of stocks, their capitalization is the same as a regular company, and may include bonds and preferred shares. Some closed-end funds are content to monitor their securities, while others play an active role in the management of the companies they hold. Canadian General Investments is an example of the former; Power Corporation of the latter. Because closed-end funds are unlikely to liquidate all their investments and distribute the proceeds to their shareholders, their shares usually trade at a *discount* to their "net asset value." (Net asset value is the break-up value of each share, and is explained in more detail later in the chapter.) The day-to-day price of closed-end fund shares is determined by market forces, not by a mathematical formula. There are less than twenty open-end funds in Canada, and they're not of much consequence to the average investor. What we're interested in for your RRSP are open-end funds.

Open-end mutual funds don't have a fixed capitalization, but continually issue and redeem their shares. Because open-end funds make their own market, they're not listed on the stock exchanges. If there's an influx of buying, the number of shares increases; if more shares are cashed-in, the number decreases. Thus the number of outstanding shares is always changing. Shares are redeemed at their net asset value. Usually there's no charge for this service, but when units are sold to an investor a fee is often added. This fee or commission is known in the industry as a "load." Fees charged at the time you buy shares are called "front-end" loads, while those charged when your units are redeemed are called "back-end" loads. If the fund doesn't charge a commission, it is described as a "no-load" fund. All mutual funds, whether they are load or no-load, charge a management fee. The management fee covers operating expenses and provides the owners of the fund with most, or all of their profit.

Open-end funds have attributes that make them particularly useful for the RRSP investor. First of all, they aim for consistent, long-term performance. With a single purchase you can get a piece of literally hundreds of companies. Depending on the fund, this can give you an instant portfolio or blanket coverage of a particular industry. Diversification not only increases your investment opportunities, but also *spreads the risk*. Added to this, your money will be looked after by experienced, professional managers—so not only will your eggs be spread among many baskets, but competent people will watch those baskets. Most open-end funds are valued daily, so it's easy to keep track of them. They're also highly liquid because you can purchase (or redeem) funds on any business day. Finally, open-end funds are convenient: they can be bought in small or odd amounts, and income can be automatically re-invested.

Mutual fund quotes are listed in the financial section of your daily newspaper. The most comprehensive fund coverage is provided by *The Financial Post,* and *The Globe and Mail.* Both publish special fund issues each month. These reports are good for comparative purposes, because performance figures go back ten years. To give you an idea of what's out there, here's a list of the fund categories in a recent *Globe* monthly report:

Asian and Pacific Rim
Canadian Bond
International Bond
Canadian Money Market
International Money Market
Canadian Equity
International Equity
U.S. Equity
Canadian Balanced
International Balanced
U.S. Balanced
Dividend
Sector Equity
Mortgage
Latin America & Emerging Markets
Precious Metals & Natural Resources

Information on funds is usually tabulated under the following headings:

- **Assets** is the size of the fund in millions of dollars (e.g., 27.5). As a general rule in Canada, the smaller the fund the more dynamic its performance, the larger the fund the greater its stability. This is due to the limited number of industrial stocks, and the thinness of our markets.

- **Fees** gives the load or commission (if any) charged to purchase the fund, and whether it is back-end or front-end—or both. We'll discuss fees and commissions in more detail later in the chapter.

- **Expense Ratio** is the total management fees, and any other costs, expressed as a percentage of the funds assets. We'll look at this too, later in the chapter.

- **RRSP** indicates whether the fund is eligible for your RRSP without resorting to the 20% foreign content allowance.

- **Volatility**, also called variability, refers to the degree of risk as measured by the price swings of the fund. The scale goes from 1 to 10, with 1 being the lowest volatility and 10 the highest. This number tells you what type of market action to expect—whether it'll be a white-knuckle ride, or a tranquil one. High growth and specialty funds tend to have above-average ratings, while balanced funds normally fall in the mid-range, and income funds have low numbers. If you're a nervous investor, stick to funds with a volatility rating of 4 or less.

- **Monthly & Yearly Returns** reflect the fund's performance for these periods. These are compounded rates, with dividends and interest re-invested, which is consistent with the investment policy of an RRSP. Use these figures to compare one fund with another, and attach the most importance to the three- and five-year terms. When zeroing in on a particular fund, check that the same management team is at the helm. And remember, *past performance is no guarantee of future performance*—it's just another measurement.

- **NAVPS** stands for "net asset value per share" and indicates the fund's intrinsic or break-up value per unit. The net asset value of the *fund* is calculated by taking the fund's assets (cash and securities) and deducting its liabilities. The net asset value per *share* is arrived at by dividing the fund's net worth by the number of outstanding shares. Here's an example:

value of securities	$37,000,000
plus cash on hand	+ $ 2,500,000
total assets	$39,500,000
less liabilities	–$ 3,200,000
fund's net worth	$36,300,000

shares outstanding 4,537,500
divide 4,537,500 into $36,300,000 = $8
net asset value per share   = $8

BALANCED FUNDS

Now let's look at the various types of funds. Balanced funds were the first to be offered in Canada. Still very popular, balanced funds consist of the three major asset classes: stocks, bonds, and cash. The proportion of each is altered according to the stage of the economic cycle. Theoretically, when the economy is expanding, equities are stressed; when it's topping out, cash is king; and when it's heading into a recession and interest rates have peaked, bonds are overweighted. Balanced portfolios usually provide above-average results, combined with reasonable safety. Although juggling investment assets to maximize returns has been around for centuries, the mutual fund industry has recently begun to market this concept under the name of "asset allocation." Accompanying their sales pitch are studies showing that shifting asset classes rather than individual securities (such as Alcan or Canadian Pacific) is the most important ingredient for success. I don't wish to be uncharitable, but I would point out that this is the *same strategy that balanced funds have always followed* (that's what "balancing" means). To date, the new asset allocation funds have performed no better than the "old fashioned" balanced funds. Which is not surprising—they're essentially the same, but sold in different wrappers.

Calling a balanced fund an "asset allocation" fund is a relatively harmless marketing ploy. However, it's ludicrous when fund dealers offer to manage on an "asset allocation" basis—for the same fee as an investment counsellor—the mutual funds in your portfolio. Let me remind you, your funds are already being managed by professionals for a fee. Aside from this service being unnecessary, you shouldn't have a grab-bag of funds in your RRSP. If you do, and some funds aren't performing up to scratch, get rid of them. All you really need to achieve asset allocation is a good Canadian balanced fund, and a balanced international fund. When new money comes in, you simply add to these two funds.

EQUITY FUNDS

Equity funds are more volatile than balanced funds because they normally hold only stocks, and a small cash reserve. Their prime objective is growth, and the little income they generate is reinvested in the fund. If you're looking for capital gain, this type of fund can provide gratifying results. It's also relatively high risk. When comparing Canadian equity funds with the idea of buying one, keep in mind the performance of the Toronto Stock Exchange 300 Index. This index, which is used to measure the overall performance of the TSE, includes a random assortment of good, bad, and indifferent listed stocks. You want to choose an equity fund that has at least matched the performance of the exchange. If you don't check this yardstick, you may end up buying the best of a bad lot. The same test can be applied to an international fund. If it's an American fund, you should look at the past record of the Dow Jones Industrial Average (the most widely followed index on the New York Stock Exchange).

So long as you can accept the risk factor, equity funds are a good route to growth. They are especially appropriate for young investors. However, for people within five years of retirement I would be inclined to substitute growth-type balanced funds for pure equity funds. That way, you'll still have an equity inflation hedge, but you won't be as vulnerable to a prolonged market downturn.

U.S. and International Equity Funds

The same advice applies to U.S. and international equity funds. U.S. funds obviously focus on one country, but international funds usually invest in a selection of countries. Some international funds invest in a particular region, such as the Pacific Rim, South America, or Europe. These regional funds can provide spectacular gains, but can also produce apalling losses. Because of their uneven performance I wouldn't put them in your RRSP. Instead, I'd suggest a fund that invests in at least twenty countries, such as one of the Templeton funds. This type of fund will provide a currency hedge as well as investment opportunities literally all over the world.

BOND FUNDS

Bond funds are the opposite to equity funds. Bond funds are structured to take advantage of interest rates. Basically, when interest rates are rising they shift to the short end, and when rates are falling they lengthen maturities. Bond funds vary in the type of debt they hold—some restrict themselves to government securities while others opt for higher yields with lower credit ratings. Whatever their investment philosophy, bond funds (except those that specialize in "junk" bonds) are essentially defensive investments. But unlike an individual bond, a bond fund never matures, so there's no guarantee that you'll get your money back. And with a bond fund, income always takes precedence over capital gain.

On balance, I don't recommend a bond fund for your RRSP (except, perhaps, an international one). Canadian bond funds have been stodgy performers for the most part, with long periods in the doldrums. I think you're better off with strip bonds.

U.S. and international bond funds offer geographic diversification and a currency hedge. The problem with U.S. bond funds is that because of the traditional interest rate spread between Canada and the States, their rate of return is always lower than Canadian bond funds. I prefer international bond funds that invest all over the world. If you scan the globe there are always countries that offer an interest rate play or a currency play—sometimes both.

MAXIMIZING FOREIGN CONTENT IN YOUR MUTUAL FUND INVESTMENTS

Recently, a number of Canadian funds have sprung up that hold Canadian bonds denominated in foreign currencies. These funds are considered to be Canadian content for your RRSP, and provide a currency hedge (because they're payable in francs, yen, Deutsche Marks, or whatever). But because the underlying bonds are all issued by the same country (Canada) they don't give any geographical diversification. They are, however, one way of getting around the foreign content restriction.

There are a couple of other ways to beat the 20% foreign content rule with mutual funds. For instance, you can buy one of the new leveraged funds that Gordon Pape has dubbed "the Pseudo Canadians." These funds typically invest 80% of their assets in Canadian Treasury Bills and other short-term securities. The remaining 20% is used to buy call options or futures on foreign stock exchange indices. In theory, these derivative investments provide the equivalent of 100% foreign equity exposure. But, because they comprise only 20% of the fund's assets, the fund still qualifies as Canadian content. So far, the performance results of the "Pseudo Canadians" has been uninspiring. Personally, leveraged derivatives make me uncomfortable, and I can't help thinking that the government will eventually close this loophole. I think they're too risky for an RRSP.

The other way you can legally increase the foreign content in your RRSP is to buy a Canadian balanced fund or an equity fund that has 20% of its assets in foreign holdings. In addition to having 20% of your RRSP in foreign securities, you can own as much of these funds as you want without breaking the limit. Theoretically, this could boost your foreign content from 20% to 36%. I see nothing wrong with this type of fund, providing it has sound management and a good track record. The easiest way to ferret out these funds is to ask your broker. That's what he's there for.

DIVIDEND FUNDS

Now let's take a look at dividend funds. Dividend funds are designed to provide good after-tax income with modest growth.

To this end, they invest a large proportion of their money in preferred shares. However, you don't care about after-tax income in your RRSP, you're only concerned with *gross* income. So I suggest you ignore dividend funds. On a gross return basis, strip bonds will outperform them any day of the week.

REAL ESTATE FUNDS

I wouldn't recommend a real estate fund for your RRSP. However, if you're young and prepared to take the risk, a real estate fund might be an interesting speculation. The reason I say this is since real estate stocks have performed so badly for so long, it's about time they perked up their weary little heads. Furthermore, despite their abysmal record, they still attract good press. Why, I do not know.

MORTGAGE FUNDS

Mortgage funds shouldn't be confused with real estate funds. Mortgage funds usually invest in first mortgages and are relatively safe. When interest rates are stable they provide above-average income with a modest potential for capital gain. For the older, more conservative investor, a good mortgage fund is a reasonable RRSP investment. Looking down the road, it can also be a useful asset in a Registered Retirement Income Fund (RRIF).

SEGREGATED FUNDS

Segregated funds are issued by life insurance companies. (Segregated refers to the fact that the underlying securities are segregated from the insurance company's other assets.) These funds are sold by insurance agents and are issued by the companies as insurance or annuity contracts. Some funds include a form of insurance that guarantees a percentage of their original value. Insurance funds are difficult to monitor as their prices are published infrequently and for some, you have to phone the company. Because each fund is different, and their performance also varies, you should always read the prospectus *before* you buy one. This is particularly true if you're considering a money market fund, because many insurance companies charge prohibitive fees.

LABOUR-SPONSORED FUNDS

Labour-sponsored funds came into existence as a result of tax legislation to promote investment in Canadian business ventures. If a person in the top income bracket buys $5000 of one of these funds he can get a 20% federal tax credit (to a maximum of $1000) and, in some provinces, an additional 20% provincial tax credit. After taking these credits he can then contribute the $5000 worth of the fund to his RRSP for its full face value. The net cost after all the tax breaks works out to something like $500.

That's the good news. The bad news is that the businesses in which these funds invest are usually unable to get money from any other source—including the banks. These businesses are bought for their *potential*, because they frequently have little or no intrinsic worth. And after the fund buys into them, you can't keep track of their value, because in most cases there's no market for them. When a venture capital company goes sour, it's often a 100% loss. For this reason, the venture capital sector is known as the graveyard of the financial business. Don't forget, too, that you are required to hold these funds for at least five to seven years, or you'll lose your tax credits. While you are locked-in, a lot of unpleasant things can happen. So make no mistake about it, a labour-sponsored fund is a high risk gamble, and *definitely not a suitable investment for your RRSP—* no matter how much the tax saving. The object of a retirement plan isn't to reduce tax today, it's to build a nest egg for tomorrow.

SECTOR EQUITY (SPECIALTY) FUNDS

Sector equity is the name for a diverse group of specialty funds. These funds invest in valuable commodities, such as precious metals, a particular industry like computers or telecommunications, or strategic resources (like oil and gas). Sector equity funds are generally volatile, and relatively high risk. Most RRSP investors can do quite satisfactorily without them.

MONEY MARKET FUNDS

Money market funds aren't a big deal, because they're only places to temporarily park your money, but there are a few things you should know about them. Money market funds invest in Treasury Bills, bonds, commercial paper and other short-term securities. Their shares, or units, usually have a par value of $10, and are *not insured*. In some cases the unit value fluctuates with interest rates—so make sure that the fund has a *fixed* unit value or you could suffer a loss of capital.

The other thing to watch out for is that some money market funds charge a front-end load or a rear-end load, or a redemption fee. Because money market yields are low, even a modest fee can ruin your return. In some cases, it can actually result in a negative return, which means you end up losing money on a supposedly safe investment. So don't, under any circumstances, buy a money market fund that charges any form of fee (other than a management fee).

Money market funds are listed separately from the other funds. They also have a slightly different format that lists two yields. Ignore "effective yield" (the compound return), because rates change daily and this is a nonsense figure. The number that counts is "current yield."

It's quite pleasant to cast your eye down the columns and by a process of elimination pick out the highest yielding fund. But, if you're shopping for your RRSP, it will probably be an academic exercise. I say this because the broker or institution that holds your plan is unlikely to go out and buy just any fund you choose. More likely, the broker will only be able to offer one or two money market funds, and have an in-house plan that pays interest on your credit balances. For practical purposes, this shouldn't be a handicap. If for some reason you're not pleased with the rates offered—and you have more than a few thousand in loose cash— simply ask your broker to buy Treasury Bills. If you have less than a few thousand, the difference isn't worth quibbling about.

COMMISSIONS

Having scanned the various types of funds, we'll now take a closer look at commissions. Some funds charge them and some funds don't. The trend is towards reducing or eliminating commissions, especially "front-end" loads, but quite a few funds still charge them. Loads are normally stated as a percentage of the net asset value. Thus, if you buy $10,000 worth of a fund and the load is 5%, you'll pay $500 commission. Front-end loads range from 9% to 2%, and are usually charged on a sliding scale. The larger the purchase the lower the sales charge. Although commissions can often be reduced at the broker's discretion, they can't be levied above a certain amount. Here's a typical front-end load schedule:

Amount of Purchase	Maximum Sales Charge
up to $9,999	9%
$10,000 to $24,999	8%
$25,000 to $49,999	6.5%
$50,000 to $99,999	5%
$100,000 to $199,999	4%
$200,000 to $299,999	3%
$300,000 to $499,999	2%
over $500,000	negotiable

Mutual funds should be regarded as a long-term investment. This is especially true if you've paid a commission, because you may need a considerable amount of time to recoup that fee. The length of time you hold your fund is also relevant for deferred or "back-end" loads. Some funds charge a flat fee of from 4% to 6%, no matter how long you hold your shares. However, the trend in back-end loads is to charge them on a sliding scale, as an incentive for you to hold the shares. Here's an example:

Length owned	Deferred or Back-end fee
less than a year	5%
2 years	4.5%
3 years	4%
4 years	3.5%
5 years	3%
6 years	2.5%
7 years and thereafter	2%

Even if it's the same percent, a rear-end load is preferable to a front-end load. With a back-end load *all your money goes to work, and compounds from the outset.* A sliding scale rear-end load is even better, in that time automatically reduces or can eliminate the sales charge. Another point to check with rear-end loads is whether the charge is made against your original cost or the current market value. It can make a difference. For instance a 4% load on a $10,000 original cost is $400; but if the value grew in the interim to $15,000 the charge would be $600. (Then again, if you made this kind of money, maybe you wouldn't mind paying a few hundred dollars more.)

From a cost point of view, a no-load fund is the best buy of all. You might wonder how a no-load fund is feasible. If they don't charge a commission, how can they make money? Let me assure you that they do make money. First of all, the cost of selling these funds is low because no sales force is maintained, and relatively little is paid in commisions to third parties. Think of the chartered banks: their regular staff also look after mutual fund sales. But the main reason no-load funds are profitable— and this applies to load funds as well—is the income they receive from their management fees.

As I mentioned earlier, management fees are expressed as ratios, and range from about 1% to 3% of the fund's assets. Fees for sector and special equity funds are at the top of the scale, closely followed by foreign funds. Most foreign funds are run on a day-to-day basis by an overseas manager. For example, a Pacific Rim fund might be managed by someone in Hong Kong or Singapore. This adds to the operating cost because there are two levels of management to pay: the people in the Far East, and the fund managers on Bay Street. Most domestic equity and balanced funds charge a management fee in the 2% range, and bond funds about half that amount. Money market funds—which require a minimum of talent to run—charge the lowest fees.

Many load funds and some no-load funds pay "trailer" commissions to salespeople for as long as their clients continue to hold the fund. These annual payments serve as an incentive to keep clients in a fund. This is very important to the fund, because fees are levied as a percentage of assets under administration—and the larger the pool of assets, the bigger the management fee. Paying trailer fees is *not* a clandestine practice (it's clearly stated in the fund's prospectus), but it could influence your broker's judgement as to whether you should sell or hold a fund. So you should be aware of it. If you want to find out if a particular fund pays trailing commissions, ask your broker straight out. He won't be embarrassed to tell you.

Load funds often defend themselves by saying that no-load funds make up the income shortfall by charging higher management fees. I used to believe this (it seemed logical) until I went to the trouble of checking several hundred Canadian funds. My conclusion was that there was little difference between the two; some no-load funds charge above-average management fees—and so do some load funds. Along with this myth, I've also heard it said that load funds consistently outperform no-load funds. From my research, this doesn't hold water either. In a recent issue of *The Globe and Mail* "Report on Mutual Funds" I discovered that of the ten top-performing mutual funds, five were load, and five were no-load. This suggests that each fund—regardless whether it's load or no-load—should be judged strictly on its own merit.

But all things being equal, I would advise you to buy a no-load fund. Most brokers will buy no-load funds for you (although there may be a small administrative fee tacked on by the firm). At the same time, don't rule out load funds. Sometimes they offer access to a special market niche, or they have a compelling performance record. In these circumstances, it makes sense to buy them. And—if you're a good client—there's no law to prevent you from asking your broker for a break on the commission. But don't go overboard trying to cut costs. You and your broker are in business together, and he has to earn a living too. What a broker—as opposed to a discount house—supplies is advice and service, and good service is worth something.

Mutual funds are core holdings in many self-directed RRSPs. For this reason they deserve your serious consideration. When I get carried away comparing management ratios, loads and no-loads, I remind myself that the purpose of investing is not to *save* money but to *make* money. Don't let administrative numbers bog you down, but keep your eye on the performance figures. This will help you to pick winners. Mutual funds are amazingly versatile and, if you choose wisely, they will reward you handsomely.

9

The Pay-Off

You can collapse your RRSP at any age, but you *must* do so by the end of the year you turn 71. At that time you have three options: you can take the cash, buy an annuity, or roll the proceeds into a Registered Retirement Income Fund (RRIF). You can also choose any combination of the three.

Annuities and income funds pay monthly, quarterly, semi-annual, or annual instalments. These disbursements are taxed as income, but the principal remains tax sheltered. However, if you decide to *cash* your RRSP the *total* proceeds will be added to your income and taxed at your marginal rate. Unless it's a very small RRSP, this means a substantial amount of your savings will go up the flue. So taking cash doesn't make much sense (unless you plan to spend your sunset years in Tahiti, and even then some retirement income would be useful). I should also mention that if you fail to take any action when you reach 71, your RRSP will suffer the same fate—it will be collapsed automatically, and the proceeds taxed.

With a locked-in RRSP or a locked-in retirement account (LIRA) the cash option is irrelevant. This type of plan can't be collapsed until you reach retirement age, which is usually 65. And when you do collapse it, you can't take the cash, nor can you roll the proceeds into a RRIF. Your only choice is to buy a life annuity, or in some provinces a Life Income Fund (LIF).

ANNUITIES

There are all sorts of annuities, and the insurance industry is continually coming up with new varieties. But when you clear away the underbrush, there are basically only two types of annuity: one that pays for life, the other until you reach a certain age. The one that pays for life is called a "life annuity" (surprise). The one that pays for a number of years—usually until age 90—is called "fixed term" or "term certain."

An annuity—whether it be for life or to age 90—is safe and provides a steady stream of income. Although you have no control over an annuity, it requires no management. Most annuities pay a level amount from start to finish, thus there's no protection against inflation. And with an annuity you're normally locked in for the full term. However, with some annuities liquidity and inflation protection (in the form of indexing) can be purchased—at a cost of substantially reduced returns.

If you compare a life annuity with a fixed term annuity, you'll see that the fixed term annuity provides a slightly higher payout for the same sum of money. But does this mean you should automatically choose fixed term? It all depends how long you think you'll live. A recent study on life expectancy indicated that one out of six Canadians who are 65 today will live to be more than 90. In view of these findings (and because fixed term ceases at 90), you shouldn't rule out a life annuity.

When buying a life annuity, there are two essential options to consider: joint survivorship and a guarantee period. A joint survivor clause ensures that if you die your spouse will inherit the annuity (and the payments will continue for the life of your spouse). A guarantee period ensures that you or your estate will receive a certain number of payments. If the guarantee is ten years, and you die after three, your estate will receive payments for seven more years, or the commuted value (which may be more or less than a multiplication of the payments). The rule of thumb on the guarantee option is to select the minimum period to recover the cost. Ten years will usually do the trick. The reason I stress *minimum* is that this is an extra, and extras cost money— the longer the guarantee, the more the payout is reduced. If you don't have a joint survivor clause or a guarantee, and you die six months after buying an annuity, your estate gets nothing.

A joint survivor clause is also useful with a fixed term annuity. (Although, if your spouse is your principal beneficiary, sometimes the balance of the annuity will be transferred automatically.) Also it's worth noting that with a fixed term annuity you won't need a guarantee clause, because the payments—or the commuted value—are guaranteed to age 90.

For those who don't want to take any risks, *except the risk of inflation*, an annuity is the logical way to fund your retirement. To get the best rate, go to an annuity broker, not your friendly insurance agent. An annuity broker isn't restricted to one company but shops the entire market—and may check fifty or sixty companies—to find you the best value.

REGISTERED RETIREMENT INCOME FUNDS (RRIFs)

A RRIF is the opposite of an RRSP. Instead of accumulating capital, a RRIF disburses the proceeds of your RRSP in instalments. Like an RRSP, assets within a RRIF are tax sheltered, but the payments you receive from it are taxed as income, the same as an annuity. The amount you receive from your RRIF each year is up to you—*subject to a minimum*. There are two formulas to calculate your minimum withdrawal. If you are less than 71, to find the amount you divide the value of your RRIF by 90 less your age. Let's say that on the first of the year you're 60, and the value of your RRIF is $120,000. Here's the calculation:

90 minus 60 (your age) = 30 divided into $120,000 = $4000

This formula applies until you reach the end of your 70th year. From age 71 on, the minimum withdrawal is expressed as a percentage of the value of your RRIF. Here are the figures:

Age	Minimum Payout
71	7.38%
72	7.48%
73	7.59%
74	7.71%
75	7.85%
76	7.99%
77	8.15%
78	8.33%
79	8.53%
80	8.75%
81	8.99%
82	9.27%
83	9.58%
84	9.93%
85	10.3%
86	10.8%
87	11.3%
88	12.0%
89	12.7%
90	13.6%
91	14.7%
92	16.1%
93	17.9%
94	20.0%
from age 95 on	20.0%

This schedule shows that even if you make minimum withdrawals, you'll still need a gross return of around 8% to avoid an immediate erosion of capital. And if you achieve constant returns of 8%, your portfolio will peak in value around your 80th birthday.

RRIF withdrawals that exceed the minimum amount are subject to federal withholding tax. (Sums withheld are, of course, credited as income tax payments.) Withholding rates increase with the amounts withdrawn. The schedule for most of the provinces is the same, except for Quebec, which also withholds provincial income tax.

If the amount withdrawn exceeds the minimum by:	withholding tax most provinces	withholding tax Quebec
up to $5000	10%	21%
$5001 to $15,000	20%	30%
more than $15,000	30%	35%

A RRIF, like an RRSP, can be bequeathed to your spouse. You can also have more than one RRIF. And, if your spouse is younger than you are, you can use your spouse's age to determine the minimum percentages. You would do this to reduce the withdrawal amounts (and thereby reduce the erosion of capital) in your RRIF.

Before delving deeper into RRIFs, let's look at their repressed cousin, the LIF (Life Income Fund). A LIF is one of two basic options for a locked-in RRSP or LIRA (Locked-in Retirement Account). A LIF is similar to a RRIF in that you have control, and the same eligible investments. And, like a RRIF, there's a minimum withdrawal each year. However, a LIF also has a *maximum* withdrawal limit. This is calculated by a formula tied to the payout of an annuity to age 90, based on a floating interest rate (the CANSIM rate) for the first 15 years, and 6% for the period thereafter. Sounds complicated? It is (and it has to be recalculated annually), but the institution that holds your LIF will crunch the numbers for you. Finally, if you have a LIF you must convert it to a life annuity by the end of the year you reach 80.

Your RRIF: Self-Directed or Managed?

You can set up a LIF or a RRIF at the same financial institution that handled your RRSP. Indeed, with a self-directed RRSP it's logical to roll it into a self-directed RRIF with the same firm. Or if you wish, you can collapse your RRSP and put the proceeds into a managed RRIF. Managed RRIFs are sold mainly by banks, trust companies and insurance companies. Most are marketed on an interest rate basis similar to an annuity. The major difference between a managed RRIF and a term certain annuity is that the RRIF is more flexible (you can get out of it). In this connection, banks and trust companies normally offer RRIFs with terms of no more than ten years; after that you have to renego-

tiate a rate for another five to ten years. Most insurance companies are willing to offer long-term rates, but will also sell RRIFs
with fixed rates as short as two to three years. *When interest rates
are low, stay with short terms; when they reverse, lock in the higher rates with an insurance company RRIF (but make sure you
shop around)!* Some insurance companies also offer RRIFs with
an equity component.

This brings up the question whether you should choose a
self-directed or a managed RRIF. Because most people are over
65 when they take out a RRIF, your age and state of health must
be taken into consideration. Both can affect your competence.
Also, are you interested in continuing to handle your investments? Some people, when they retire, want to keep in touch
with the business world while others prefer to travel and attend
to their hobbies. If you're not sure whether you want to get
involved with investment decisions, choose a managed RRIF.
Down the road, if you change your mind, you can collapse it and
roll the proceeds into a self-directed RRIF.

If you opt for a self-directed RRIF, give serious thought to the
contents of your portfolio. Keep in mind that there's going to be an
increasing drain on it. As a strategy, try to make the income of your
RRIF offset your withdrawals. To achieve this—and it will only be
possible for for a limited number of years—you'll need a high proportion of income investments. At the same time, you'll need to
keep some equity investments to soften the bite of inflation.

Some investments are more suitable for RRIFs than others. A
basic requirement is that they be *marketable*, because eventually they'll all be sold. This rules out personal mortgages—your
own, or anybody else's—even though they are insured. It also
rules out shares in a labour-sponsored venture capital fund. And
speaking of shares, it's not feasible to sell odd lots of listed stocks
to finance withdrawals (such as 28 shares of Laidlaw or 19 shares
of Alcan). The reason I say this is that minimum commissions
will make the sales prohibitively expensive. However, high yielding common stocks, especially banks and utilities, can be excellent core holdings for a RRIF. GICs with their maturities
staggered—so that a certain amount comes due each year—
work well in RRIFs, as do "packages" of high-grade bonds with
staggered maturities. Strip bonds, purchased in "ladders," are

perhaps the most useful of all. With a little forethought, you can buy a ladder of coupons that will look after a large percentage of your withdrawals for a good number of years.

Mutual funds are as useful in a RRIF as they are in an RRSP. Funds with low volatility are particularly well suited to RRIFs. (Low volatility funds are stolid performers who neither hit the heights nor plumb the depths.) There's a huge variety of funds to choose from—whether you're looking for income from a bond or mortgage fund, a currency hedge from an international bond fund, or asset allocation through a balanced fund. You can buy quality no-load funds in every category and, most important, most can be liquidated in small amounts at little or no cost.

RRIFs OR ANNUITIES: WHICH IS BEST FOR YOU?

Which should you buy, a RRIF or an annuity? A RRIF is more flexible, because you can alter the withdrawals, and collapse it whenever you wish. It also gives you an element of control over your financial destiny, because you can manage it yourself. With a RRIF, especially a self-directed one, you have a chance to offset the erosion of capital with a measure of growth. If you die before your capital runs out, the balance of your RRIF can be left to your spouse, or to your estate. In either case, there's something left. On the negative side, there's always the danger (unless it's a guaranteed RRIF) that you'll run out of money sooner than you expected.

An annuity provides a sum you can count on for life or at least until you reach 90. However, unless its indexed, it doesn't provide any protection against inflation (and indexing sharply reduces the payout). With a life annuity, unless you have a guarantee and you die within that period, there's no residual value. When all is said and done, the most appealing thing about an annuity is that you can count on a steady income. Unfortunately, with the passage of time, the amount you receive may prove inadequate.

What you do with the proceeds of your RRSP is a personal decision—and each person's situation is different. But whatever you do, try to delay collapsing your RRSP as long as possible. The longer your RRSP remains intact the more time your nest egg has to grow. If you have an adequate pension, I would roll the entire proceeds of your RRSP into a RRIF. And if you have substantial outside investments, I would suggest the same thing. It's an entirely different matter if you don't have a pension, and you don't want to take any risk. Under these circumstances, if long-term interest rates are in the double digits, I might put half in a life annuity and the other half in a managed RRIF. In this connection, if you don't have a spouse or other dependent, choose an annuity with no frills—it'll pay considerably more. Later on, if you want, you can convert the RRIF into another annuity. In the meantime, you'll have a pool of capital to draw on if you need it. That's the beauty of a RRIF—it can be used to your advantage in a number of ways.

Finally, don't plan your retirement hastily. Before you make any decisions, go over your priorities and income requirments. After you've got it clear in your own mind what you need *then* sit down with a professional, such as an annuity broker, and go over your options. Take your time and think about them before you commit yourself. After all, you want these to be your golden years.

Glossary

ACCOUNT ADVISOR—see BROKER.

ACCOUNT EXECUTIVE—see BROKER.

ACCRUED INTEREST—interest on a bond that has accumulated since the last payment date.

AFTER MARKET—trading of a new issue after a public offering. Supply and demand determine price levels, which often differ from the initial offering price.

AMEX—also known as the ASE, which stands for the American Stock Exchange. Located in New York, it is the second largest exchange in the United States.

ANNUITANT—person who receives an annuity (see next entry).

ANNUITY—a contract issued by an insurance company for a lump sum that pays you a fixed amount at regular intervals for the length of your life or until a certain age. Annuities may be "DEFERRED" so that payments commence months or years after the purchase.

ASSET MIX—the distribution within a portfolio of stocks, bonds and cash. Also referred to as ASSET ALLOCATION.

ASSIGN—when you write a call option and it is exercised you are assigned the security, which means you must deliver the shares.

AVERAGE DOWN—a strategy to reduce the average cost of a security by buying more units as the price declines. Should only be done if the outlook for the company remains bright.

BALANCE SHEET—a financial statement that shows a company's assets, liabilities, and net worth.

BANK OF CANADA—established 1934. Regulates the credit and currency of the country, and exerts control over the relative value of the Canadian dollar.

BANK RATE—the rate at which the Bank of Canada will lend money to the chartered banks, which is 25 basis points above the 91-day Treasury Bill rate.

BASIS POINT—one one hundredth of one percent. If a yield rises from 7.28% to 7.38% the increase is 10 basis points.

BEAR—a person who believes the market or a security will decline. See BULL.

BENEFICIARY—the heir to an RRSP, RRIF, or annuity.

BLUE CHIP—a large company that is a leader in its industry, with a consistent record of earnings and dividends.

BOARD LOT—standard trading unit for listed shares. The number of shares is determined by the stock exchange and varies with the price of the stock. See ODD LOT.

BOND—a debt security backed by a pledge of assets. See DEBENTURE.

BOOK VALUE—total tangible assets minus all liabilities and the par value of preferred shares. To get the book value per share, divide the number of common shares into this figure.

BROKER—an individual who trades securities for clients. Also refers to a stock broking firm.

BULL—one who believes the market or a security will go up. See BEAR.

CALL OPTION—a security that gives the owner the right to buy the shares of a company at a fixed price for a fixed period of time.

CALLABLE—a security that can be redeemed by the issuer before the maturity date.

CARRY FORWARD—the amount of a person's unused RRSP contribution limit. May be carried forward for seven years.

CASH FLOW—the sum of net income plus deferred taxes plus non-cash charges (such as amortization, depreciation, and depletion).

CHARTIST—one who uses a technical approach to forecast security prices.

CHICAGO BOARD OF TRADE—oldest and largest commodity exchange on the continent. Also North America's largest option market.

CHURNING—excessive trading of a client's account to generate commissions. Difficult to prove.

CIRCUIT BREAKER—regulations that prevent certain types of trading on the exchanges after the market has moved a given amount in either direction. Purpose is to dampen market swings and reduce volatility.

COMMON SHARES—see next entry, COMMON STOCK.

COMMON STOCK—represents the equity or ownership of a company. Common shareholders normally have voting rights and, by this means, control the management of the company.

COMMUTED ANNUITY—annuity that has been cashed in; the amount may be more or less that the sum of future payments.

CONTRIBUTION LIMIT—the maximum amount you are allowed to contribute to your RRSP.

CONVERTIBLE—usually refers to bonds or preferred shares that may be converted into common shares.

COUPON—the interest rate expressed as a percentage of the face value of the security, e.g., a 6 percent coupon on a bond. Also refers to small cashable certificates representing interest instalments that are attached to "coupon" bonds.

(Coupons are sometimes stripped from a certificate and sold at a discount).

COVERED WRITING—the sale of call options on a security that you own.

DEBENTURE—a form of long-term debt similar to a bond, but secured by the general credit of the issuer rather than specific assets.

DEBT/EQUITY RATIO—calculated by adding long-term debt and preferred shares, and dividing the total by the net worth of the common shares.

DEBT INSTRUMENT—any type of debt security, e.g., bonds, debentures, T-Bills, GICs, mortgages, etc.

DEFERRED PROFIT SHARING PLAN (DPSP)—a registered plan in which profits are shared by the company with the employees.

DEPLETION—accounting allowance for the amount of oil or ore drawn from a well or a mine.

DEPRECIATION—accounting allowance representing the reduction in value of an asset (such as a building or a piece of machinery), through wear and tear or obsolescence.

DERIVATIVE—security derived from another financial instrument. Options, rights, warrants, strip bonds, split shares, stock receipts, etc. are all derivatives.

DISCRETIONARY ACCOUNT—an account for which the client gives the broker *written* authority to make investment decisions on the client's behalf. Should only be done after careful consideration of the possible consequences.

DIVIDEND—cash distribution, usually quarterly, to common and preferred shareholders made at the discretion of the board of directors.

DIVIDEND TAX CREDIT—only applicable to shares of Canadian companies. Canadian residents "gross-up" and inflate the dividend by 25% and then deduct 13½% of that amount from tax payable. This credit does *not* apply to shares in an RRSP or a RRIF.

DOW JONES INDUSTRIAL AVERAGE—an average composed of 30 senior stocks on the New York Stock Exchange. Usually referred to simply as "The Dow" (although it is only one of a number of Dow averages).

EARNED INCOME—in respect to an RRSP, income that is eligible for the calculation of your maximum contrution.

EARNINGS PER SHARE—often expressed as EPS, calculated by dividing the company's net earnings (after dividends on any preferred shares) by the number of outstanding common shares.

FINANCIAL ADVISOR—one of several euphemisms for BROKER. Because it implies professionalism, this title is also used by some mutual fund salespeople.

FOREIGN CONTENT—in respect to an RRSP or a RRIF, applies to non-Canadian issuers of securities, except for certain supranational organizations. The *book* value of your foreign content may not exceed 20% of the book value of the total portfolio. (Although the *market* value can exceed this percentage.)

GIC—stands for Guaranteed Investment Certificate, which is a deposit note bearing interest for a fixed term.

HOME BUYERS PLAN—a program that permits first-time home buyers to withdraw, tax-free, up to $20,000 from their RRSP to fund their purchase. Money withdrawn must be repaid over a period of fifteen years or it is taxed as a straight withdrawal.

HOT ISSUE—a security offering that is oversubscribed and goes to an immediate premium. Brokers usually reserve these issues for their good clients.

IDA—stands for the Investment Dealers Association of Canada. Founded in 1916, this is the self-regulating body of the Canadian securities industry.

INSTITUTIONAL INVESTOR—industry term for large investors such as pension funds, insurance companies, banks, and mutual funds.

INTEGRATED OIL—refers to the vertical integration of an oil company. An integrated oil company does everything from exploration through to the selling of refined products at its own gas stations.

INVESTMENT ADVISOR—see BROKER.

INVESTMENT GRADE SECURITIES—high quality stocks or bonds.

LEAP—acronym for long-term stock option. This type of option has a term of one or two years rather than the normal nine months.

LEVERAGE—using a small amount of money to get the play off a larger amount. Rights, warrants, and options are a few examples of leveraged securities.

LIFE INCOME FUND (LIF)—a retirement option for those with locked-in RRSPs. Similar in some respects, but more restrictive than a RRIF.

LIQUIDITY—the ability of an investment to be turned into cash. The quicker this can be done, the more liquid the security.

LOCKED-IN RRSP—one that must be converted to an annuity or a Life Income Fund upon retirement, and cannot be cashed.

MARGINAL TAX RATE—the highest rate of tax that you pay on your income.

NET ASSET VALUE—the intrinsic value of a share or unit in a mutual fund. Calculated by dividing the number of units in the fund into the fund's net worth. Often referred to as NAV.

NET WORTH—the amount by which a company's assets exceed its liabilities. Also called "shareholders' equity."

NEW YORK STOCK EXCHANGE—founded in 1792, the largest and best known stock exchange on this continent.

ODD LOT—any number of shares that differs from a standard trading unit or BOARD LOT.

OPEC—acronym for Organization of Petroleum Exporting Countries.

OVERCONTRIBUTION—sum contributed to your RRSP in excess of the allowed amount. You may overcontribute a maximum of $2000.

OVER-THE-COUNTER—a securities market where dealers trade among themselves by telephone, telex, and computer, rather than on a stock exchange. Also known as the UNLISTED MARKET.

PAPER PROFIT—the profit in a security that has not yet been liquidated. The opposite is a "paper loss."

PAR VALUE—the face value of a bond or preferred share. Means nothing when applied to common shares.

PEAC—acronym for payment enhanced capital security; the portion of a split common share that receives the dividend income.

PENSION ADJUSTMENT (PA)—the amount of pension contribution benefits you have received from your employer. This figure (your PA) is used to calculate how much you can contribute to your RRSP.

PRICE/EARNINGS RATIO—to calculate this ratio divide the earnings per share into the price of the stock.

PRIME RATE—the rate of interest the chartered banks charge their best customers.

PRO FORMA—a Latin phrase used to describe financial projections in a prospectus, after applying the proceeds of the issue.

PROSPECTUS—a legal document that provides detailed information on a securities issue. Tedious but important reading.

PUT OPTION—security that gives you the right to sell a given number of shares at a fixed price for a specified period of time.

REGISTERED REPRESENTATIVE—correct name for a licensed securities salesperson. See BROKER.

RETRACTABLE PREFERRED—a preferred share that gives the holder the right to have it redeemed by the issuer on a certain date at a specified price.

RIGHT OF RECISSION—legal right to cancel purchase of a new issue if it has been misrepresented in the prospectus.

RIGHTS OFFERING—privilege extended to existing shareholders to purchase additional shares on a pro rata basis at a discount from the current market price. If a shareholder doesn't want to subscribe, the rights usually have some value and can be sold.

RISK/REWARD RATIO—the potential loss versus the potential gain in a contemplated trade. If you could lose $5 but make $15, the ratio would be 1 to 3. Used mainly to assess speculative transactions.

ROLLOVER—either the automatic re-investment of an income investment, such as a GIC or a Treasury Bill, or the tax sheltered transfer of retirement savings into an annuity or RRIF.

RRIF—acronym for Registered Retirement Income Fund.

RRSP—acronym for Registered Retirement Savings Plan.

SECONDARY OFFERING—the sale of a block of securities to the public by the existing holder. The proceeds go to the vendor, not into the treasury of the company.

SELF-DIRECTED RRSP—a registered retirement savings plan that is managed by the holder.

SHARE—an equity unit in a company. See also COMMON STOCK.

SINKING FUND—a pool of money set aside by a company for the purchase of its outstanding bonds or preferred shares.

SPEC—acronym for special equity claim security; the growth portion of a split share.

SPLIT SHARE—a common share that is divided into two parts. One part receives all the dividends, the other part the price appreciation. See PEAC and SPEC.

SPOUSAL RRSP—a retirement plan funded by a person for his or her spouse.

STANDARD & POOR'S—well known American financial service.

STOCK SPLIT—the subdivision of existing shares into smaller units, e.g., a 3 for 1 split triples the number of shares you own. A share split doesn't increase your percentage of ownership, it merely increases the number of shares.

STRIKE PRICE—the price at which an option may be exercised.

STRIP—to detach the coupons from a bond, and market each one separately at a discount from their face value. Also a common name for a zero coupon security. See also ZERO COUPON BOND.

SYNDICATE—in the financial sense, a group of investment dealers who underwrite a securities issue. The syndicate buys the entire issue, and is also responsible for marketing it.

TAXABLE INCOME—the amount of money remaining, after deductions, that is subject to tax.

THRIFT INSTITUTION—colloquial name for a bank, trust company, credit union, or caisse populaire.

TREASURY BILL—a short-term obligation of the Government of Canada. Most T-Bills have a term of 91 days, but they can also have a term of up to 2 years. They do not bear interest. Their yield comes from the difference between the discount at which they're purchased and their face value at maturity.

UNDERWRITE—in the investment sense, the process whereby one or more dealers purchase an issue of securities. Until the issue is sold to the public, the underwriters are normally at risk for the entire amount.

UNIT—either a share in a mutual fund or a security consisting of more than one component (for example, a new issue composed of one common share and one stock purchase warrant).

VARIABLE RATE—an income security with a fluctuating rate of return that is tied to another interest rate, or to an index. There are countless variable rate formulas.

VESTED BENEFIT—a pension or profit sharing contribution made by the employer that belongs to the employee.

VOLATILITY—the more violently a security fluctuates in price, the greater the risk. Conversely, the more stable it is, the greater the safety.

WARRANT—has two meanings: either a long term right, or a certificate for rights.

WORKING CAPITAL—the amount remaining after current liabilities have been deducted from current assets.

WRITE—when applied to options, means the sale of a put or a call.

YIELD—the return, expressed as a percentage, of a security.

ZERO COUPON BOND—a bond that has been stripped of its coupons. Both the stripped bond (the principal) and the coupons are sold to investors. Because neither the bond nor the coupons pay interest, they are sold at a discount. The return on zero coupon securities is derived from the difference between their cost and their face value at maturity.

Index